MW00984943

The Law School Admission Council (LSAC) is a nonprofit corporation that provides unique, state-of-the-art admission products and services to ease the admission process for law schools and their applicants worldwide. Currently, 222 law schools in the United States, Canada, and Australia are members of the Council and benefit from LSAC's services.

ISBN-13: 978-0-9983397-0-2

Print number
10 9 8 7 6 5 4 3 2 1

# TABLE OF CONTENTS

# INTRODUCTION TO THE LSAT

The Law School Admission Test is a half-day standardized test required for admission to all ABA-approved law schools, most Canadian law schools, and many other law schools. It consists of five 35-minute sections of multiple-choice questions. Four of the five sections contribute to the test taker's score. These sections include one Reading Comprehension section, one Analytical Reasoning section, and two Logical Reasoning sections. The unscored section, commonly referred to as the variable section, typically is used to pretest new test questions or to preequate new test forms. The placement of this section in the LSAT will vary. A 35-minute writing sample is administered at the end of the test. The writing sample is not scored by LSAC, but copies are sent to all law schools to which you apply. The score scale for the LSAT is 120 to 180.

The LSAT is designed to measure skills considered essential for success in law school: the reading and comprehension of complex texts with accuracy and insight; the organization and management of information and the ability to draw reasonable inferences from it; the ability to think critically; and the analysis and evaluation of the reasoning and arguments of others.

The LSAT provides a standard measure of acquired reading and verbal reasoning skills that law schools can use as one of several factors in assessing applicants.

For up-to-date information about LSAC's services, go to our website, LSAC.org.

## SCORING

Your LSAT score is based on the number of questions you answer correctly (the raw score). There is no deduction for incorrect answers, and all questions count equally. In other words, there is no penalty for guessing.

### Test Score Accuracy—Reliability and Standard Error of Measurement

Candidates perform at different levels on different occasions for reasons quite unrelated to the characteristics of a test itself. The accuracy of test scores is best described by the use of two related statistical terms: reliability and standard error of measurement.

**Reliability** is a measure of how consistently a test measures the skills being assessed. The higher the reliability coefficient for a test, the more certain we can be that test takers would get very similar scores if they took the test again.

LSAC reports an internal consistency measure of reliability for every test form. Reliability can vary from 0.00 to 1.00, and a test with no measurement error would have a reliability coefficient of 1.00 (never attained in practice). Reliability coefficients for past LSAT forms have ranged from .90 to .95, indicating a high degree of consistency for these tests. LSAC expects the reliability of the LSAT to continue to fall within the same range.

LSAC also reports the amount of measurement error associated with each test form, a concept known as the standard error of measurement (SEM). The SEM, which is usually about 2.6 points, indicates how close a test taker's observed score is likely to be to his or her true score. True scores are theoretical scores that would be obtained from perfectly reliable tests with no measurement error—scores never known in practice.

Score bands, or ranges of scores that contain a test taker's true score a certain percentage of the time, can be derived using the SEM. LSAT score bands are constructed by adding and subtracting the (rounded) SEM to and from an actual LSAT score (e.g., the LSAT score, plus or minus 3 points). Scores near 120 or 180 have asymmetrical bands. Score bands constructed in this manner will contain an individual's true score approximately 68 percent of the time.

Measurement error also must be taken into account when comparing LSAT scores of two test takers. It is likely that small differences in scores are due to measurement error rather than to meaningful differences in ability. The standard error of score differences provides some guidance as to the importance of differences between two scores. The standard error of score differences is approximately 1.4 times larger than the standard error of measurement for the individual scores.

Thus, a test score should be regarded as a useful but approximate measure of a test taker's abilities as measured by the test, not as an exact determination of his or her abilities. LSAC encourages law schools to examine the range of scores within the interval that probably contains the test taker's true score (e.g., the test taker's score band) rather than solely interpret the reported score alone.

### Adjustments for Variation in Test Difficulty

All test forms of the LSAT reported on the same score scale are designed to measure the same abilities, but one test form may be slightly easier or more difficult than another. The scores from different test forms are made comparable through a statistical procedure known as equating. As a result of equating, a given scaled score earned on different test forms reflects the same level of ability.

### Research on the LSAT

Summaries of LSAT validity studies and other LSAT research can be found in member law school libraries and at LSAC.org.

## To Inquire About Test Questions

If you find what you believe to be an error or ambiguity in a test question that affects your response to the question, contact LSAC by e-mail: LSATTS@LSAC.org, or write to Law School Admission Council, Test Development Group, PO Box 40, Newtown, PA 18940-0040.

## HOW THIS PREPTEST DIFFERS FROM AN ACTUAL LSAT

This PrepTest is made up of the scored sections and writing sample from the actual disclosed LSAT administered in December 2016. However, it does not contain the extra, variable section that is used to pretest new test items of one of the three multiple-choice question types. The three multiple-choice question types may be in a different order in an actual LSAT than in this PrepTest. This is because the order of these question types is intentionally varied for each administration of the test.

## THE THREE LSAT MULTIPLE-CHOICE QUESTION TYPES

The multiple-choice questions that make up most of the LSAT reflect a broad range of academic disciplines and are intended to give no advantage to candidates from a particular academic background.

The five sections of the test contain three different question types. The following material presents a general discussion of the nature of each question type and some strategies that can be used in answering them.

### Analytical Reasoning Questions

Analytical Reasoning questions are designed to assess the ability to consider a group of facts and rules, and, given those facts and rules, determine what could or must be true. The specific scenarios associated with these questions are usually unrelated to law, since they are intended to be accessible to a wide range of test takers. However, the skills tested parallel those involved in determining what could or must be the case given a set of regulations, the terms of a contract, or the facts of a legal case in relation to the law. In Analytical Reasoning questions, you are asked to reason deductively from a set of statements and rules or principles that describe relationships among persons, things, or events.

Analytical Reasoning questions appear in sets, with each set based on a single passage. The passage used for each set of questions describes common ordering relationships or grouping relationships, or a combination of both types of relationships. Examples include scheduling employees for work shifts, assigning instructors to class sections, ordering tasks according to priority, and distributing grants for projects.

Analytical Reasoning questions test a range of deductive reasoning skills. These include:

- Comprehending the basic structure of a set of relationships by determining a complete solution to the problem posed (for example, an acceptable seating arrangement of all six diplomats around a table)

- Reasoning with conditional ("if-then") statements and recognizing logically equivalent formulations of such statements

- Inferring what could be true or must be true from given facts and rules

- Inferring what could be true or must be true from given facts and rules together with new information in the form of an additional or substitute fact or rule

- Recognizing when two statements are logically equivalent in context by identifying a condition or rule that could replace one of the original conditions while still resulting in the same possible outcomes

Analytical Reasoning questions reflect the kinds of detailed analyses of relationships and sets of constraints that a law student must perform in legal problem solving. For example, an Analytical Reasoning passage might describe six diplomats being seated around a table, following certain rules of protocol as to who can sit where. You, the test taker, must answer questions about the logical implications of given and new information. For example, you may be asked who can sit between diplomats X and Y, or who cannot sit next to X if W sits next to Y. Similarly, if you were a student in law school, you might be asked to analyze a scenario involving a set of particular circumstances and a set of governing rules in the form of constitutional provisions, statutes, administrative codes, or prior rulings that have been upheld. You might then be asked to determine the legal options in the scenario: what is required given the scenario, what is permissible given the scenario, and what is prohibited given the scenario. Or you might be asked to develop a "theory" for the case: when faced with an incomplete set of facts about the case, you must fill in the picture based on what is implied by the facts that are known. The problem could be elaborated by the addition of new information or hypotheticals.

No formal training in logic is required to answer these questions correctly. Analytical Reasoning questions are intended to be answered using knowledge, skills, and reasoning ability generally expected of college students and graduates.

## Suggested Approach

Some people may prefer to answer first those questions about a passage that seem less difficult and then those that seem more difficult. In general, it is best to finish one passage before starting on another, because much time can be lost in returning to a passage and reestablishing familiarity with its relationships. However, if you are having great difficulty on one particular set of questions and are spending too much time on them, it may be to your advantage to skip that set of questions and go on to the next passage, returning to the problematic set of questions after you have finished the other questions in the section.

Do not assume that because the conditions for a set of questions look long or complicated, the questions based on those conditions will be especially difficult.

**Read the passage carefully.** Careful reading and analysis are necessary to determine the exact nature of the relationships involved in an Analytical Reasoning passage. Some relationships are fixed (for example, P and R must always work on the same project). Other relationships are variable (for example, Q must be assigned to either team 1 or team 3). Some relationships that are not stated explicitly in the conditions are implied by and can be deduced from those that are stated (for example, if one condition about paintings in a display specifies that Painting K must be to the left of Painting Y, and another specifies that Painting W must be to the left of Painting K, then it can be deduced that Painting W must be to the left of Painting Y).

In reading the conditions, do not introduce unwarranted assumptions. For instance, in a set of questions establishing relationships of height and weight among the members of a team, do not assume that a person who is taller than another person must weigh more than that person. As another example, suppose a set involves ordering and a question in the set asks what must be true if both X and Y must be earlier than Z; in this case, do not assume that X must be earlier than Y merely because X is mentioned before Y. All the information needed to answer each question is provided in the passage and the question itself.

The conditions are designed to be as clear as possible. Do not interpret the conditions as if they were intended to trick you. For example, if a question asks how many people could be eligible to serve on a committee, consider only those people named in the passage unless directed otherwise. When in doubt, read the conditions in their most obvious sense. Remember, however, that the language in the conditions is intended to be read for precise meaning. It is essential to pay particular attention to words that describe or limit relationships, such as "only," "exactly," "never," "always," "must be," "cannot be," and the like.

The result of this careful reading will be a clear picture of the structure of the relationships involved, including the kinds of relationships permitted, the participants in the relationships, and the range of possible actions or attributes for these participants.

**Keep in mind question independence.** Each question should be considered separately from the other questions in its set. No information, except what is given in the original conditions, should be carried over from one question to another.

In some cases a question will simply ask for conclusions to be drawn from the conditions as originally given. Some questions may, however, add information to the original conditions or temporarily suspend or replace one of the original conditions for the purpose of that question only. For example, if Question 1 adds the supposition "if P is sitting at table 2 ...," this supposition should NOT be carried over to any other question in the set.

**Consider highlighting text and using diagrams.** Many people find it useful to underline key points in the passage and in each question. In addition, it may prove very helpful to draw a diagram to assist you in finding the solution to the problem.

In preparing for the test, you may wish to experiment with different types of diagrams. For a scheduling problem, a simple calendar-like diagram may be helpful. For a grouping problem, an array of labeled columns or rows may be useful.

Even though most people find diagrams to be very helpful, some people seldom use them, and for some individual questions no one will need a diagram. There is by no means universal agreement on which kind of diagram is best for which problem or in which cases a diagram is most useful. Do not be concerned if a particular problem in the test seems to be best approached without the use of a diagram.

## Logical Reasoning Questions

Arguments are a fundamental part of the law, and analyzing arguments is a key element of legal analysis. Training in the law builds on a foundation of basic reasoning skills. Law students must draw on the skills of analyzing, evaluating, constructing, and refuting arguments. They need to be able to identify what information is relevant to an issue or argument and what impact further evidence might have. They need to be able to reconcile opposing positions and use arguments to persuade others.

Logical Reasoning questions evaluate the ability to analyze, critically evaluate, and complete arguments as they occur in ordinary language. The questions are based on short arguments drawn from a wide variety of sources, including newspapers, general interest magazines, scholarly publications, advertisements, and informal discourse. These arguments mirror legal reasoning in the types of arguments presented and in their complexity, though few of the arguments actually have law as a subject matter.

Each Logical Reasoning question requires you to read and comprehend a short passage, then answer one question (or, rarely, two questions) about it. The questions are designed to assess a wide range of skills involved in thinking critically, with an emphasis on skills that are central to legal reasoning.

These skills include:

- Recognizing the parts of an argument and their relationships

- Recognizing similarities and differences between patterns of reasoning

- Drawing well-supported conclusions

- Reasoning by analogy

- Recognizing misunderstandings or points of disagreement

- Determining how additional evidence affects an argument

- Detecting assumptions made by particular arguments

- Identifying and applying principles or rules

- Identifying flaws in arguments

- Identifying explanations

The questions do not presuppose specialized knowledge of logical terminology. For example, you will not be expected to know the meaning of specialized terms such as "ad hominem" or "syllogism." On the other hand, you will be expected to understand and critique the reasoning contained in arguments. This requires that you possess a university-level understanding of widely used concepts such as argument, premise, assumption, and conclusion.

## Suggested Approach

Read each question carefully. Make sure that you understand the meaning of each part of the question. Make sure that you understand the meaning of each answer choice and the ways in which it may or may not relate to the question posed.

Do not pick a response simply because it is a true statement. Although true, it may not answer the question posed.

Answer each question on the basis of the information that is given, even if you do not agree with it. Work within the context provided by the passage. LSAT questions do not involve any tricks or hidden meanings.

## Reading Comprehension Questions

Both law school and the practice of law revolve around extensive reading of highly varied, dense, argumentative, and expository texts (for example, cases, codes, contracts, briefs, decisions, evidence). This reading must be exacting, distinguishing precisely what is said from what is not said. It involves comparison, analysis, synthesis, and application (for example, of principles and rules). It involves drawing appropriate inferences and applying ideas and arguments to new contexts. Law school reading also requires the ability to grasp unfamiliar subject matter and the ability to penetrate difficult and challenging material.

The purpose of LSAT Reading Comprehension questions is to measure the ability to read, with understanding and insight, examples of lengthy and complex materials similar to those commonly encountered in law school. The Reading Comprehension section of the LSAT contains four sets of reading questions, each set consisting of a selection of reading material followed by five to eight questions. The reading selection in three of the four sets consists of a single reading passage; the other set contains two related shorter passages. Sets with two passages are a variant of Reading Comprehension called Comparative Reading, which was introduced in June 2007.

Comparative Reading questions concern the relationships between the two passages, such as those of generalization/instance, principle/application, or point/counterpoint. Law school work often requires reading two or more texts in conjunction with each other and understanding their relationships. For example, a law student may read a trial court decision together with an appellate court decision that overturns it, or identify the fact pattern from a hypothetical suit together with the potentially controlling case law.

Reading selections for LSAT Reading Comprehension questions are drawn from a wide range of subjects in the humanities, the social sciences, the biological and physical sciences, and areas related to the law. Generally, the selections are densely written, use high-level vocabulary, and contain sophisticated argument or complex rhetorical structure (for example, multiple points of view). Reading Comprehension questions require you to read carefully and accurately, to determine the relationships among the various parts of the reading selection, and to draw reasonable inferences from the material in the selection. The questions may ask about the following characteristics of a passage or pair of passages:

- The main idea or primary purpose

- Information that is explicitly stated

- Information or ideas that can be inferred

- The meaning or purpose of words or phrases as used in context

- The organization or structure

- The application of information in the selection to a new context

- Principles that function in the selection

- Analogies to claims or arguments in the selection

- An author's attitude as revealed in the tone of a passage or the language used

- The impact of new information on claims or arguments in the selection

## Suggested Approach

Since reading selections are drawn from many different disciplines and sources, you should not be discouraged if you encounter material with which you are not familiar. It is important to remember that questions are to be answered exclusively on the basis of the information provided in the selection. There is no particular knowledge that you are expected to bring to the test, and you should not make inferences based on any prior knowledge of a subject that you may have. You may, however, wish to defer working on a set of questions that seems particularly difficult or unfamiliar until after you have dealt with sets you find easier.

**Strategies.** One question that often arises in connection with Reading Comprehension has to do with the most effective and efficient order in which to read the selections and questions. Possible approaches include:

- reading the selection very closely and then answering the questions;

- reading the questions first, reading the selection closely, and then returning to the questions; or

- skimming the selection and questions very quickly, then rereading the selection closely and answering the questions.

Test takers are different, and the best strategy for one might not be the best strategy for another. In preparing for the test, therefore, you might want to experiment with the different strategies and decide what works most effectively for you.

Remember that your strategy must be effective under timed conditions. For this reason, the first strategy—reading the selection very closely and then answering the questions—may be the most effective for you. Nonetheless, if you believe that one of the other strategies

might be more effective for you, you should try it out and assess your performance using it.

**Reading the selection.** Whatever strategy you choose, you should give the passage or pair of passages at least one careful reading before answering the questions. Try to distinguish main ideas from supporting ideas, and opinions or attitudes from factual, objective information. Note transitions from one idea to the next and identify the relationships among the different ideas or parts of a passage, or between the two passages in Comparative Reading sets. Consider how and why an author makes points and draws conclusions. Be sensitive to implications of what the passages say.

You may find it helpful to mark key parts of passages. For example, you might underline main ideas or important arguments, and you might circle transitional words—"although," "nevertheless," "correspondingly," and the like—that will help you map the structure of a passage. Also, you might note descriptive words that will help you identify an author's attitude toward a particular idea or person.

## Answering the Questions

- Always read all the answer choices before selecting the best answer. The best answer choice is the one that most accurately and completely answers the question being posed.

- Respond to the specific question being asked. Do not pick an answer choice simply because it is a true statement. For example, picking a true statement might yield an incorrect answer to a question in which you are asked to identify an author's position on an issue, since you are not being asked to evaluate the truth of the author's position but only to correctly identify what that position is.

- Answer the questions only on the basis of the information provided in the selection. Your own views, interpretations, or opinions, and those you have heard from others, may sometimes conflict with those expressed in a reading selection; however, you are expected to work within the context provided by the reading selection. You should not expect to agree with everything you encounter in Reading Comprehension passages.

## THE WRITING SAMPLE

On the day of the test, you will be asked to write one sample essay. LSAC does not score the writing sample, but copies are sent to all law schools to which you apply. According to a 2015 LSAC survey of 129 United States and Canadian law schools, almost all utilize the writing sample in evaluating some applications for admission. Failure to respond to writing sample prompts and frivolous responses have been used by law schools as grounds for rejection of applications for admission.

In developing and implementing the writing sample portion of the LSAT, LSAC has operated on the following premises: First, law schools and the legal profession value highly the ability to communicate effectively in writing. Second, it is important to encourage potential law students to develop effective writing skills. Third, a sample of an applicant's writing, produced under controlled conditions, is a potentially useful indication of that person's writing ability. Fourth, the writing sample can serve as an independent check on other writing submitted by applicants as part of the admission process. Finally, writing samples may be useful for diagnostic purposes related to improving a candidate's writing.

The writing prompt presents a decision problem. You are asked to make a choice between two positions or courses of action. Both of the choices are defensible, and you are given criteria and facts on which to base your decision. There is no "right" or "wrong" position to take on the topic, so the quality of each test taker's response is a function not of which choice is made, but of how well or poorly the choice is supported and how well or poorly the other choice is criticized.

The LSAT writing prompt was designed and validated by legal education professionals. Since it involves writing based on fact sets and criteria, the writing sample gives applicants the opportunity to demonstrate the type of argumentative writing that is required in law school, although the topics are usually nonlegal.

You will have 35 minutes in which to plan and write an essay on the topic you receive. Read the topic and the accompanying directions carefully. You will probably find it best to spend a few minutes considering the topic and organizing your thoughts before you begin writing. In your essay, be sure to develop your ideas fully, leaving time, if possible, to review what you have written. Do not write on a topic other than the one specified. Writing on a topic of your own choice is not acceptable.

No special knowledge is required or expected for this writing exercise. Law schools are interested in the reasoning, clarity, organization, language usage, and writing mechanics displayed in your essay. How well you write is more important than how much you write. Confine your essay to the blocked, lined area on the front and back of the separate Writing Sample Response Sheet. Only that area will be reproduced for law schools. Be sure that your writing is legible.

## TAKING THE PREPTEST UNDER SIMULATED LSAT CONDITIONS

One important way to prepare for the LSAT is to simulate the day of the test by taking a practice test under actual time constraints. Taking a practice test under timed conditions helps you to estimate the amount of time you can afford to spend on each question in a section and to determine the question types on which you may need additional practice.

Since the LSAT is a timed test, it is important to use your allotted time wisely. During the test, you may work only on the section designated by the test supervisor. You cannot devote extra time to a difficult section and make up that time on a section you find easier. In pacing yourself, and checking your answers, you should think of each section of the test as a separate minitest.

Be sure that you answer every question on the test. When you do not know the correct answer to a question, first eliminate the responses that you know are incorrect, then make your best guess among the remaining choices. Do not be afraid to guess as there is no penalty for incorrect answers.

When you take a practice test, abide by all the requirements specified in the directions and keep strictly within the specified time limits. Work without a rest period. When you take an actual test, you will have only a short break—usually 10–15 minutes—after SECTION III.

When taken under conditions as much like actual testing conditions as possible, a practice test provides very useful preparation for taking the LSAT.

Official directions for the four multiple-choice sections and the writing sample are included in this PrepTest so that you can approximate actual testing conditions as you practice.

To take the test:

- Set a timer for 35 minutes. Answer all the questions in SECTION I of this PrepTest. Stop working on that section when the 35 minutes have elapsed.

- Repeat, allowing yourself 35 minutes each for sections II, III, and IV.

- Set the timer again for 35 minutes, then prepare your response to the writing sample topic at the end of this PrepTest.

- Refer to "Computing Your Score" for the PrepTest for instruction on evaluating your performance. An answer key is provided for that purpose.

**The practice test that follows consists of four sections corresponding to the four scored sections of the December 2016 LSAT. Also reprinted is the December 2016 unscored writing sample topic.**

# General Directions for the LSAT Answer Sheet

The actual testing time for this portion of the test will be 2 hours 55 minutes. There are five sections, each with a time limit of 35 minutes. The supervisor will tell you when to begin and end each section. If you finish a section before time is called, you may check your work on that section **only**; do not turn to any other section of the test book and do not work on any other section either in the test book or on the answer sheet.

There are several different types of questions on the test, and each question type has its own directions. **Be sure you understand the directions for each question type before attempting to answer any questions in that section.**

Not everyone will finish all the questions in the time allowed. Do not hurry, but work steadily and as quickly as you can without sacrificing accuracy. You are advised to use your time effectively. If a question seems too difficult, go on to the next one and return to the difficult question after completing the section. **MARK THE BEST ANSWER YOU CAN FOR EVERY QUESTION. NO DEDUCTIONS WILL BE MADE FOR WRONG ANSWERS. YOUR SCORE WILL BE BASED ONLY ON THE NUMBER OF QUESTIONS YOU ANSWER CORRECTLY.**

**ALL YOUR ANSWERS MUST BE MARKED ON THE ANSWER SHEET.** Answer spaces for each question are lettered to correspond with the letters of the potential answers to each question in the test book. After you have decided which of the answers is correct, blacken the corresponding space on the answer sheet. **BE SURE THAT EACH MARK IS BLACK AND COMPLETELY FILLS THE ANSWER SPACE.** Give only one answer to each question. If you change an answer, be sure that all previous marks are **erased completely.** Since the answer sheet is machine scored, incomplete erasures may be interpreted as intended answers. **ANSWERS RECORDED IN THE TEST BOOK WILL NOT BE SCORED.**

There may be more question numbers on this answer sheet than there are questions in a section. Do not be concerned, but be certain that the section and number of the question you are answering matches the answer sheet section and question number. Additional answer spaces in any answer sheet section should be left blank. Begin your next section in the number one answer space for that section.

LSAC takes various steps to ensure that answer sheets are returned from test centers in a timely manner for processing. In the unlikely event that an answer sheet is not received, LSAC will permit the examinee either to retest at no additional fee or to receive a refund of his or her LSAT fee. **THESE REMEDIES ARE THE ONLY REMEDIES AVAILABLE IN THE UNLIKELY EVENT THAT AN ANSWER SHEET IS NOT RECEIVED BY LSAC.**

## Score Cancellation

Complete this section only if you are absolutely certain you want to cancel your score. **A CANCELLATION REQUEST CANNOT BE RESCINDED. IF YOU ARE AT ALL UNCERTAIN, YOU SHOULD NOT COMPLETE THIS SECTION.**

To cancel your score from this administration, you **must:**

A. fill in both ovals here ...... ◯ ◯

**AND**

B. read the following statement. Then sign your name and enter the date. **YOUR SIGNATURE ALONE IS NOT SUFFICIENT FOR SCORE CANCELLATION. BOTH OVALS ABOVE MUST BE FILLED IN FOR SCANNING EQUIPMENT TO RECOGNIZE YOUR REQUEST FOR SCORE CANCELLATION.**

I certify that I wish to cancel my test score from this administration. I understand that my request is irreversible and that my score will not be sent to me or to the law schools to which I apply.

Sign your name in full

Date

**FOR LSAC USE ONLY** ◯

## HOW DID YOU PREPARE FOR THE LSAT?
### (Select all that apply.)

**Responses to this item are voluntary and will be used for statistical research purposes only.**

◯ By studying the free sample questions available on LSAC's website.
◯ By taking the free sample LSAT available on LSAC's website.
◯ By working through official LSAT *PrepTests*, *ItemWise*, and/or other LSAC test prep products.
◯ By using LSAT prep books or software **not** published by LSAC.
◯ By attending a commercial test preparation or coaching course.
◯ By attending a test preparation or coaching course offered through an undergraduate institution.
◯ Self study.
◯ Other preparation.
◯ No preparation.

## CERTIFYING STATEMENT

Please write the following statement. Sign and date.

I certify that I am the examinee whose name appears on this answer sheet and that I am here to take the LSAT for the sole purpose of being considered for admission to law school. I further certify that I will neither assist nor receive assistance from any other candidate, and I agree not to copy, retain, or transmit examination questions in any form or discuss them with any other person.

_____
_____
_____
_____
_____
_____
_____
_____
_____

SIGNATURE: _____  TODAY'S DATE: ___/___/___
                                        MONTH  DAY  YEAR

INSTRUCTIONS FOR COMPLETING THE BIOGRAPHICAL AREA ARE ON THE BACK COVER OF YOUR TEST BOOKLET.
**USE ONLY A NO. 2 OR HB PENCIL TO COMPLETE THIS ANSWER SHEET. DO NOT USE INK.**

**A**

**1 LAST NAME / FIRST NAME / MI**

(A–Z bubble grid for each letter position)

**2 LAST 4 DIGITS OF SOCIAL SECURITY/ SOCIAL INSURANCE NO.**  L

(0–9 bubble grid)

**3 LSAC ACCOUNT NUMBER**

(0–9 bubble grid)

**4 CENTER NUMBER**

(0–9 bubble grid)

**5 DATE OF BIRTH**

| MONTH | DAY | YEAR |
|-------|-----|------|
| ○ Jan | | |
| ○ Feb | | |
| ○ Mar | (0)(0)(0) | (0)(0) |
| ○ Apr | (1)(1)(1) | (1)(1) |
| ○ May | (2)(2)(2) | (2)(2) |
| ○ June | (3)(3)(3) | (3)(3) |
| ○ July | (4)(4) | (4)(4) |
| ○ Aug | (5)(5) | (5)(5) |
| ○ Sept | (6)(6) | (6)(6) |
| ○ Oct | (7)(7) | (7)(7) |
| ○ Nov | (8)(8) | (8)(8) |
| ○ Dec | (9)(9) | (9)(9) |

**6 TEST FORM CODE**

(0–9 bubble grid)

**7 RACIAL/ETHNIC DESCRIPTION Mark one or more**

- ○ 1 Amer. Indian/Alaska
- ○ 2 Asian
- ○ 3 Black/African Ame
- ○ 4 Canadian Aborigi
- ○ 5 Caucasian/White
- ○ 6 Hispanic/Latino
- ○ 7 Native Hawaiian/ Other Pacific Islan
- ○ 8 Puerto Rican
- ○ 9 TSI/Aboriginal Au

**8 SEX**
- ○ Male
- ○ Female

**9 DOMINANT LANGUAGE**
- ○ English
- ○ Other

**10 ENGLISH FLUENCY**
- ○ Yes
- ○ No

**11 TEST DATE**

/ /

MONTH  DAY  YEAR

**12 TEST FORM**

## Law School Admission Test

Mark one and only one answer to each question. Be sure to fill in completely the space for your intended answer choice. If you erase, do so completely. Make no stray marks.

**13 TEST BOOK SERIAL NO.**

(A–T and 0–9 bubble grid)

| SECTION 1 | SECTION 2 | SECTION 3 | SECTION 4 | SECTION 5 |
|-----------|-----------|-----------|-----------|-----------|
| 1 (A)(B)(C)(D)(E) | 1 (A)(B)(C)(D)(E) | 1 (A)(B)(C)(D)(E) | 1 (A)(B)(C)(D)(E) | 1 (A)(B)(C)(D)(E) |
| 2 (A)(B)(C)(D)(E) | 2 (A)(B)(C)(D)(E) | 2 (A)(B)(C)(D)(E) | 2 (A)(B)(C)(D)(E) | 2 (A)(B)(C)(D)(E) |
| 3 (A)(B)(C)(D)(E) | 3 (A)(B)(C)(D)(E) | 3 (A)(B)(C)(D)(E) | 3 (A)(B)(C)(D)(E) | 3 (A)(B)(C)(D)(E) |
| 4 (A)(B)(C)(D)(E) | 4 (A)(B)(C)(D)(E) | 4 (A)(B)(C)(D)(E) | 4 (A)(B)(C)(D)(E) | 4 (A)(B)(C)(D)(E) |
| 5 (A)(B)(C)(D)(E) | 5 (A)(B)(C)(D)(E) | 5 (A)(B)(C)(D)(E) | 5 (A)(B)(C)(D)(E) | 5 (A)(B)(C)(D)(E) |
| 6 (A)(B)(C)(D)(E) | 6 (A)(B)(C)(D)(E) | 6 (A)(B)(C)(D)(E) | 6 (A)(B)(C)(D)(E) | 6 (A)(B)(C)(D)(E) |
| 7 (A)(B)(C)(D)(E) | 7 (A)(B)(C)(D)(E) | 7 (A)(B)(C)(D)(E) | 7 (A)(B)(C)(D)(E) | 7 (A)(B)(C)(D)(E) |
| 8 (A)(B)(C)(D)(E) | 8 (A)(B)(C)(D)(E) | 8 (A)(B)(C)(D)(E) | 8 (A)(B)(C)(D)(E) | 8 (A)(B)(C)(D)(E) |
| 9 (A)(B)(C)(D)(E) | 9 (A)(B)(C)(D)(E) | 9 (A)(B)(C)(D)(E) | 9 (A)(B)(C)(D)(E) | 9 (A)(B)(C)(D)(E) |
| 10 (A)(B)(C)(D)(E) | 10 (A)(B)(C)(D)(E) | 10 (A)(B)(C)(D)(E) | 10 (A)(B)(C)(D)(E) | 10 (A)(B)(C)(D)(E) |
| 11 (A)(B)(C)(D)(E) | 11 (A)(B)(C)(D)(E) | 11 (A)(B)(C)(D)(E) | 11 (A)(B)(C)(D)(E) | 11 (A)(B)(C)(D)(E) |
| 12 (A)(B)(C)(D)(E) | 12 (A)(B)(C)(D)(E) | 12 (A)(B)(C)(D)(E) | 12 (A)(B)(C)(D)(E) | 12 (A)(B)(C)(D)(E) |
| 13 (A)(B)(C)(D)(E) | 13 (A)(B)(C)(D)(E) | 13 (A)(B)(C)(D)(E) | 13 (A)(B)(C)(D)(E) | 13 (A)(B)(C)(D)(E) |
| 14 (A)(B)(C)(D)(E) | 14 (A)(B)(C)(D)(E) | 14 (A)(B)(C)(D)(E) | 14 (A)(B)(C)(D)(E) | 14 (A)(B)(C)(D)(E) |
| 15 (A)(B)(C)(D)(E) | 15 (A)(B)(C)(D)(E) | 15 (A)(B)(C)(D)(E) | 15 (A)(B)(C)(D)(E) | 15 (A)(B)(C)(D)(E) |
| 16 (A)(B)(C)(D)(E) | 16 (A)(B)(C)(D)(E) | 16 (A)(B)(C)(D)(E) | 16 (A)(B)(C)(D)(E) | 16 (A)(B)(C)(D)(E) |
| 17 (A)(B)(C)(D)(E) | 17 (A)(B)(C)(D)(E) | 17 (A)(B)(C)(D)(E) | 17 (A)(B)(C)(D)(E) | 17 (A)(B)(C)(D)(E) |
| 18 (A)(B)(C)(D)(E) | 18 (A)(B)(C)(D)(E) | 18 (A)(B)(C)(D)(E) | 18 (A)(B)(C)(D)(E) | 18 (A)(B)(C)(D)(E) |
| 19 (A)(B)(C)(D)(E) | 19 (A)(B)(C)(D)(E) | 19 (A)(B)(C)(D)(E) | 19 (A)(B)(C)(D)(E) | 19 (A)(B)(C)(D)(E) |
| 20 (A)(B)(C)(D)(E) | 20 (A)(B)(C)(D)(E) | 20 (A)(B)(C)(D)(E) | 20 (A)(B)(C)(D)(E) | 20 (A)(B)(C)(D)(E) |
| 21 (A)(B)(C)(D)(E) | 21 (A)(B)(C)(D)(E) | 21 (A)(B)(C)(D)(E) | 21 (A)(B)(C)(D)(E) | 21 (A)(B)(C)(D)(E) |
| 22 (A)(B)(C)(D)(E) | 22 (A)(B)(C)(D)(E) | 22 (A)(B)(C)(D)(E) | 22 (A)(B)(C)(D)(E) | 22 (A)(B)(C)(D)(E) |
| 23 (A)(B)(C)(D)(E) | 23 (A)(B)(C)(D)(E) | 23 (A)(B)(C)(D)(E) | 23 (A)(B)(C)(D)(E) | 23 (A)(B)(C)(D)(E) |
| 24 (A)(B)(C)(D)(E) | 24 (A)(B)(C)(D)(E) | 24 (A)(B)(C)(D)(E) | 24 (A)(B)(C)(D)(E) | 24 (A)(B)(C)(D)(E) |
| 25 (A)(B)(C)(D)(E) | 25 (A)(B)(C)(D)(E) | 25 (A)(B)(C)(D)(E) | 25 (A)(B)(C)(D)(E) | 25 (A)(B)(C)(D)(E) |
| 26 (A)(B)(C)(D)(E) | 26 (A)(B)(C)(D)(E) | 26 (A)(B)(C)(D)(E) | 26 (A)(B)(C)(D)(E) | 26 (A)(B)(C)(D)(E) |
| 27 (A)(B)(C)(D)(E) | 27 (A)(B)(C)(D)(E) | 27 (A)(B)(C)(D)(E) | 27 (A)(B)(C)(D)(E) | 27 (A)(B)(C)(D)(E) |
| 28 (A)(B)(C)(D)(E) | 28 (A)(B)(C)(D)(E) | 28 (A)(B)(C)(D)(E) | 28 (A)(B)(C)(D)(E) | 28 (A)(B)(C)(D)(E) |
| 29 (A)(B)(C)(D)(E) | 29 (A)(B)(C)(D)(E) | 29 (A)(B)(C)(D)(E) | 29 (A)(B)(C)(D)(E) | 29 (A)(B)(C)(D)(E) |
| 30 (A)(B)(C)(D)(E) | 30 (A)(B)(C)(D)(E) | 30 (A)(B)(C)(D)(E) | 30 (A)(B)(C)(D)(E) | 30 (A)(B)(C)(D)(E) |

**14 PLEASE PRINT INFORMATION**

LAST NAME

FIRST NAME

DATE OF BIRTH

# THE PREPTEST

- Logical Reasoning ............................................SECTION I
- Reading Comprehension.................................SECTION II
- Analytical Reasoning........................................SECTION III
- Logical Reasoning .............................................SECTION IV
- Writing Sample Materials

SECTION I

Time—35 minutes

25 Questions

<u>Directions</u>: The questions in this section are based on the reasoning contained in brief statements or passages. For some questions, more than one of the choices could conceivably answer the question. However, you are to choose the <u>best</u> answer; that is, the response that most accurately and completely answers the question. You should not make assumptions that are by commonsense standards implausible, superfluous, or incompatible with the passage. After you have chosen the best answer, blacken the corresponding space on your answer sheet.

1. In a recent study of dust-mite allergy sufferers, one group slept on mite-proof bedding, while a control group slept on bedding that was not mite-proof. The group using mite-proof bedding had a 69 percent reduction in the dust-mite allergen in their mattresses, whereas there was no significant reduction in the control group. However, even though bedding is the main source of exposure to dust mites, no symptom reduction was reported in either group.

Which one of the following, if true, most helps to resolve the apparent conflict in the statements above?

(A)　Dust-mite allergens in bedding tend to irritate many allergy sufferers' nasal passages more than do the same allergens in other locations, such as carpets.

(B)　When people report their own allergy symptoms, they tend to exaggerate the severity of those symptoms.

(C)　The medical community does not fully understand how dust-mite allergens cause allergy.

(D)　For dust-mite allergy sufferers to get relief from their allergies, dust-mite allergens must be reduced by 90 to 95 percent.

(E)　All of the participants in the study were told that one group in the study would be sleeping on mite-proof bedding.

2. Five years ago, the hair dryer produced by the Wilson Appliance Company accounted for 50 percent of all sales of hair dryers nationwide. Currently, however, Wilson Appliance's product makes up only 25 percent of such sales. Because of this decline, and because the average net income that Wilson receives per hair dryer sold has not changed over the last 5 years, the company's net income from sales of the product must be only half of what it was 5 years ago.

The reasoning in the argument is flawed because the argument

(A)　mistakes a decline in the market share of Wilson Appliance's hair dryer for a decline in the total sales of that product

(B)　does not provide specific information about the profits hair dryers generate for the companies that produce them

(C)　fails to discuss sales figures for Wilson Appliance's products other than its hair dryers

(D)　overlooks the possibility that the retail price of Wilson Appliance's hair dryer may have increased over the past 5 years

(E)　provides no independent evidence that Wilson Appliance's hair dryer is one of the company's least profitable products

GO ON TO THE NEXT PAGE.

3. Whether or not one can rightfully call a person's faithfulness a virtue depends in part on the object of that person's faithfulness. Virtues are by definition praiseworthy, which is why no one considers resentment virtuous, even though it is in fact a kind of faithfulness— faithfulness to hatreds or animosities.

Which one of the following most accurately expresses the overall conclusion drawn in the argument?

(A) The object of a person's faithfulness partially determines whether or not that faithfulness is virtuous.

(B) Virtuous behavior is praiseworthy by definition.

(C) Behavior that emerges from hatred or animosity cannot be called virtuous.

(D) Faithfulness and resentment are obviously different, despite some similarities.

(E) Resentment should not be considered a virtuous emotion.

4. Columnist: A government-owned water utility has received approval to collect an additional charge on water bills and to use that additional revenue to build a dam. A member of the legislature has proposed not building the dam but instead spending the extra money from water bills to build new roads. That proposal is unacceptable.

Which one of the following principles, if valid, most helps to justify the columnist's judgment that the legislator's proposal is unacceptable?

(A) Customers of a utility have a right to know how the money they pay to the utility will be used.

(B) Money designated for projects that benefit an entire community should not be used for projects that benefit only some members of a community.

(C) An additional charge on water bills should not be used to fund a project that most of the utility's customers disapprove of.

(D) An additional charge on water bills should not be imposed unless it is approved by the legislature.

(E) A water utility should not collect an additional charge unless the money collected is used for water-related expenditures.

5. During its caterpillar stage, the leopard magpie moth feeds on a plant called the Natal grass cycad and by so doing laces its body with macrozamin, a toxin that makes the moth highly unpalatable to would-be predators. Since the Natal grass cycad is now endangered and facing extinction, the leopard magpie moth is also in danger of extinction.

Which one of the following is an assumption required by the argument?

(A) Feeding on the Natal grass cycad is the only means by which the leopard magpie moth can make itself highly unpalatable to predators.

(B) The leopard magpie moth does not have the speed or the agility to escape from any of its potential predators.

(C) Potential predators of the leopard magpie moth cannot determine from appearance alone whether a moth's body is laced with macrozamin.

(D) Leopard magpie moths are not able to locate Natal grass cycads unless those plants are abundant.

(E) None of the potential predators of the leopard magpie moth have developed a tolerance to macrozamin.

GO ON TO THE NEXT PAGE.

6.  Citizen: Our government has a large budget surplus, which our leaders wish to use to pay down the national debt. This makes no sense. Because of underfunding, our military is inadequate, the infrastructures of our cities are decaying, and our highways are in disrepair. If homeowners used all their money to pay off their mortgages early, while refusing to pay for upkeep of their homes, this would not make them better off financially. The same goes for the country as a whole.

Which one of the following most accurately expresses the conclusion drawn in the citizen's argument?

(A) Homeowners should not pay off their mortgages early if they must neglect upkeep of their homes in order to do so.

(B) It does not make sense for the government to use the budget surplus to pay down the national debt.

(C) A homeowner's personal financial situation is analogous in relevant ways to the financial situation of a country's government.

(D) Because of underfunding, the government does not maintain adequate standards in the services it provides.

(E) Government leaders want to use the country's large budget surplus to pay down the national debt.

7.  Peraski: Although driving gas-guzzling automobiles produces a greater level of pollution than driving smaller cars, those of us who drive smaller cars when we could use a bicycle cannot speak out against the use of gas guzzlers. We would be revealing our hypocrisy.

Jackson: I acknowledge I could do better in this area. But, it would be worse not to speak out against greater sources of pollution just because I am being hypocritical.

The dialogue provides the most support for the claim that Peraski and Jackson disagree over whether

(A) driving a gas-guzzling automobile produces a greater level of pollution than driving a smaller car

(B) speaking out against the use of gas guzzlers despite driving in situations in which one could use a bicycle reveals hypocrisy

(C) driving even a small car when one could use a bicycle contributes to the level of pollution

(D) one should speak out against polluting even if doing so reveals one's own hypocrisy

(E) there is no moral difference between driving a gas guzzler and driving a smaller car

8.  For a species of large abalone shellfish to develop from a species of smaller ones, they must spend less energy on finding food and avoiding predators, and more on competition in mating. So it is surprising that the fossil record shows that a species of large abalones developed from a smaller one only after otters, which prey on abalones, began to dominate the waters in which the abalones lived.

Which one of the following, if true, most helps to resolve the apparent discrepancy in the information above?

(A) Otters and abalones also compete for the same types of food and so are drawn to the same waters.

(B) The fossils that were studied showed the development of only one of the two species of large abalones known to exist.

(C) Otters also prey on the abalones' competitors for food and so indirectly make it easier for abalones to get food.

(D) Small abalone species tend to reproduce more rapidly than larger abalone species.

(E) Otters have a preference for large abalones over small ones and so prefer waters in which large abalones are found.

9.  Some managers think that the best way to maximize employee performance is to institute stiff competition among employees. However, in situations where one competitor is perceived to be clearly superior, other competitors become anxious and doubt their own ability to perform. Thus, stiff competition can undermine the result it was intended to achieve.

The conclusion of the argument can be properly drawn if which one of the following is assumed?

(A) Those who are perceived to be clearly superior almost always win.

(B) The winner of a competition is often the competitor who exerts the most effort.

(C) When competitors perceive the competition as winnable, their overall performance generally improves.

(D) Doubting one's own ability to perform can decrease one's overall performance.

(E) Competitors who work to undermine the confidence of other participants often do better in competitions.

GO ON TO THE NEXT PAGE.

10. Creating a database of all the plant species in the scientific record has proved to be no easy task. For centuries, botanists have been collecting and naming plants without realizing that many were in fact already named. And by using DNA analysis, botanists have shown that varieties of plants long thought to belong to the same species actually belong to different species.

Of the following claims, which one can most justifiably be rejected on the basis of the statements above?

(A) Most of the duplicates and omissions among plant names in the scientific record have yet to be cleared up.

(B) An accurate database of all the plant species in the scientific record can serve as an aid to botanists in their work.

(C) Duplicates and omissions in the scientific record also occur in fields other than botany.

(D) Botanists have no techniques for determining whether distinct plant species have been given distinct names.

(E) A person who consults the scientific record looking under only one of a plant's names may miss available information about that plant.

11. A year ago several regional hospitals attempted to reduce the number of patient injuries resulting from staff errors by implementing a plan to systematically record all such errors. The incidence of these injuries has substantially decreased at these hospitals since then. Clearly, the knowledge that their errors were being carefully monitored made the hospitals' staffs much more meticulous in carrying out their patient-care duties.

Which one of the following, if true, most strengthens the argument?

(A) Before the plan was implemented the hospitals already had a policy of thoroughly investigating any staff error that causes life-threatening injury to a patient.

(B) The incidence of patient injuries at a regional hospital that did not participate in the plan also decreased over the year in question.

(C) The plan did not call for the recording of staff errors that could have caused patient injuries but did not.

(D) The decrease in the incidence of the injuries did not begin at any hospital until the staff there became aware that the records were being closely analyzed.

(E) Under the plan, the hospitals' staff members who were found to have made errors that caused injuries to patients received only reprimands for their first errors.

12. In a national park located on an island, a herd of moose was increasing in number and threatening to destroy species of native plants. Wolves were introduced to the island to reduce the herd and thereby prevent destruction of the vegetation. Although the wolves prospered, the moose herd continued to grow.

Which one of the following, if true, most helps to explain the failure of the strategy involving wolves?

(A) The presence of wolves in an area tends to discourage other predators from moving into the area.

(B) Attempts to control moose populations in other national parks by introducing predators have also been unsuccessful.

(C) Wolves often kill moose weakened by diseases that probably would have spread to other moose.

(D) Healthy moose generally consume more vegetation than do those that are diseased or injured.

(E) Moose that are too old to breed are just as likely to die of natural causes as of attack by wolves.

13. If the purpose of laws is to contribute to people's happiness, we have a basis for criticizing existing laws as well as proposing new laws. Hence, if that is not the purpose, then we have no basis for the evaluation of existing laws, from which we must conclude that existing laws acquire legitimacy simply because they are the laws.

The reasoning in the argument is flawed in that the argument

(A) takes a sufficient condition for a state of affairs to be a necessary condition for it

(B) infers a causal relationship from the mere presence of a correlation

(C) trades on the use of a term in one sense in a premise and in a different sense in the conclusion

(D) draws a conclusion about how the world actually is on the basis of claims about how it should be

(E) infers that because a set of things has a certain property, each member of that set has the property

GO ON TO THE NEXT PAGE.

14. In order for life to exist on the recently discovered planet P23, there must be water on the planet's surface. But there is no water on P23's surface, so there is no life on planet P23.

The pattern of reasoning in the argument above is most similar to that in which one of the following arguments?

(A) A company must have efficient employees to be successful. And if a company's employees are knowledgeable and hardworking, then they are probably efficient. Thus, in order for a company to be successful, it must have knowledgeable and hardworking employees.

(B) The fact that the suspect was flustered when questioned by the police might be a result of the suspect's surprise at being questioned. But if it is, the probability that the suspect is guilty is very low. Thus, the fact that the suspect was flustered is not necessarily a sign that the suspect is guilty.

(C) Oil companies are not buying new drilling equipment. But if they were planning on increasing their drilling, they would be buying new drilling equipment. Thus, oil companies are not planning on increasing their drilling.

(D) The price of real estate in a particular town is increasing. And if the town's economy were improving, the price of real estate there would increase. Thus, the town's economy is improving.

(E) The exports of a particular nation have recently decreased. But whenever that nation's exports decrease, its trade deficit increases. Thus, the nation's trade deficit has recently increased.

15. Sanchez: The sixteen new computers that the school purchased were not as expensive as many people assume. So it isn't true that too much was spent on computers.

Merriweather: It isn't that the school paid more for each computer than it was worth, but that the computers that were purchased were much more elaborate than they needed to be.

The dialogue provides the most support for the claim that Sanchez and Merriweather disagree over whether the school

(A) needed sixteen new computers
(B) purchased more computers than it should have
(C) spent more in purchasing the sixteen computers than it should have
(D) paid more for each computer than it was worth
(E) has been harshly criticized for purchasing the sixteen computers

16. Airport administrator: According to the latest figures, less than 1 commercial flight in 2 million strays off course while landing, a number low enough to allow runways to be built closer together without a significant increase in risk. Opponents of closer runways claim that the number is closer to 1 in 20,000, but this figure is based on a partial review of air traffic control tapes and so is relatively unreliable compared to the other figure, which is based on a thorough study of the flight reports required of pilots for all commercial flights.

Which one of the following most accurately describes a flaw in the airport administrator's argument?

(A) The argument presumes, without providing justification, that building runways closer together will encourage pilots to be more cautious while landing.

(B) The argument overlooks the fact that those who make mistakes are often unreliable sources of information about those mistakes.

(C) The argument questions the integrity of those who are opposed to allowing runways to be built closer together.

(D) The argument presumes, without providing justification, that the air traffic control tapes studied do not provide accurate information concerning specific flights.

(E) The argument infers from a lack of conclusive evidence supporting the higher number's accuracy that it must be inaccurate.

GO ON TO THE NEXT PAGE.

17. In deep temperate lakes, water temperatures vary according to depth. In winter, the coldest water is at the top; in summer, at the bottom. The changes in temperature distribution, or "turnover," occur in fall and late winter. Lake trout will be found, as a rule, in the coldest water. So, if anglers seek lake trout in deep temperate lakes while these lakes are partially iced over in late winter, they will do best to eschew the lake trout's summer haunts and fish instead in a shallow bay or close to the surface off a rocky point.

Which one of the following is an assumption on which the argument depends?

(A) The ease with which lake trout can be caught by anglers varies with the time of year and the water temperature.
(B) Cold water is denser, and therefore heavier, than relatively warmer water.
(C) Lake trout are found exclusively in deep temperate lakes.
(D) Lake trout do not alter their feeding habits from one part of the year to another.
(E) In deep temperate lakes that have ice residues on the surface, late-winter "turnover" has not yet occurred.

18. Liang: Watching movies in which violence is portrayed as an appropriate way to resolve problems increases levels of aggression in viewers. Therefore, children's access to these movies should be restricted.

Sarah: Watching a drama whose characters are violent allows the audience to vicariously experience the emotions associated with aggression and thus be purged of them. Hence, the access by mature audiences to such forms of entertainment should not be restricted.

The dialogue provides the most support for inferring that Liang and Sarah agree with each other that

(A) people who experience an emotion vicariously are likely to purge themselves of that emotion
(B) the members of a mature audience are unlikely to believe that violence is sometimes an appropriate way to resolve problems
(C) if violence in certain movies causes violence in viewers, access to those movies should be restricted
(D) the effects of dramatic depictions of violence on audiences are at least partially understood
(E) children are more likely than adults to be attracted to dramas involving characters who behave violently

19. Politician: Of the candidates running, Thompson is the best person to lead this nation. For one thing, Thompson opposes higher taxes whereas the other candidates support them. Many would agree that anyone who opposes higher taxes will make a better leader than someone who supports them.

Which one of the following, if true, casts the most doubt on the politician's argument?

(A) Opposing higher taxes is not a factor contributing to good leadership.
(B) Being opposed to higher taxes is not a sufficient condition for good leadership.
(C) Thompson has questionable opinions concerning important issues other than taxes.
(D) All of the past leaders who supported higher taxes performed their jobs adequately.
(E) All of the past leaders who supported higher taxes were hardworking.

20. Patterson: Bone flutes dating to the Upper Paleolithic are the earliest evidence for music. Thus it is likely that music first arose during this period.

Garza: But the Upper Paleolithic is exceptional for the intensive use of bone, which typically survives well in archaeological contexts, unlike other materials commonly used for musical instruments, such as wood.

Garza responds to Patterson by doing which one of the following?

(A) arguing that the body of evidence to which Patterson appeals is insufficient for Patterson's purposes
(B) offering evidence to challenge the truth of the premise of Patterson's argument
(C) presenting a counterexample to the general conclusion drawn in Patterson's argument
(D) presenting an argument analogous to Patterson's argument to reveal a potential flaw in Patterson's reasoning
(E) using Patterson's evidence to draw a conclusion inconsistent with the conclusion drawn in Patterson's argument

GO ON TO THE NEXT PAGE.

21. No occupation should be subject to a licensing requirement unless incompetence in the performance of tasks normally carried out within that occupation poses a plausible threat to human health or safety.

The principle stated above, if valid, most helps to justify the reasoning in which one of the following arguments?

(A) Because some of the duties that police officers carry out have no connection to human health or safety, police officers should not be subject to a licensing requirement.

(B) Because there are no realistic circumstances in which poor work by an interior designer poses a danger to human beings, interior designers should not be subject to a licensing requirement.

(C) Because hospital administrators routinely make decisions that affect the health of hundreds of people, hospital administrators should be subject to a licensing requirement.

(D) Because hair stylists regularly use substances that can pose a threat to human health if handled improperly, hair stylists should be subject to a licensing requirement.

(E) Because tattoo artists who do not maintain strict sanitation pose a serious threat to human health, tattoo artists should be subject to a licensing requirement.

22. Most of the new cars that Regis Motors sold last year were purchased by residents of Blomenville. Regis Motors sold more new cars last year than it did in any previous year. Still, most new cars purchased by Blomenville residents last year were not purchased from Regis Motors.

If the statements above are true, which one of the following must also be true?

(A) Regis Motors sold more new cars to residents of Blomenville last year than they had in any previous year.

(B) The total number of new cars purchased by residents of Blomenville was greater last year than it was in any previous year.

(C) A car retailer other than Regis Motors sold the most new cars to residents of Blomenville last year.

(D) The number of new cars purchased last year by residents of Blomenville is greater than the number of new cars sold by Regis Motors.

(E) Regis Motors' share of the new car market in Blomenville last year increased over its share the year before.

23. Editorial: Teenagers tend to wake up around 8:00 A.M., the time when they stop releasing melatonin, and are sleepy if made to wake up earlier. Since sleepiness can impair driving ability, car accidents involving teenagers driving to school could be reduced if the school day began later than 8:00 A.M. Indeed, when the schedule for Granville's high school was changed so that school began at 8:30 A.M. rather than earlier, the overall number of car accidents involving teenage drivers in Granville declined.

Which one of the following, if true, provides the most support for the argument in the editorial?

(A) Teenagers start releasing melatonin later at night and stop releasing it later in the morning than do young children.

(B) Sleepy teenagers are tardy for school more frequently than teenagers who are well rested when the school day begins.

(C) Teenagers who work at jobs during the day spend more time driving than do teenagers who attend high school during the day.

(D) Many of the car accidents involving teenage drivers in Granville occurred in the evening rather than in the morning.

(E) Car accidents involving teenage drivers rose in the region surrounding Granville during the time they declined in Granville.

GO ON TO THE NEXT PAGE.

24. Lucinda will soon be attending National University as an engineering major. At National University, most residents of Western Hall are engineering majors. Therefore, Lucinda will probably live in Western Hall.

Which one of the following arguments exhibits a flawed pattern of reasoning most similar to that exhibited by the argument above?

(A) A major shopping mall is now being constructed in our city. Most cities with major shopping malls are regional economic hubs. Therefore, our city will probably become a regional economic hub.

(B) Cities that are regional economic hubs generally experience tremendous economic growth at some point. Our city is a regional economic hub that has never experienced tremendous economic growth. Thus it will probably experience tremendous economic growth in the future.

(C) Cities that are regional economic hubs always have excellent transportation systems. It is widely agreed that our city's transportation system is inadequate. Therefore, our city will probably never become a regional economic hub.

(D) A major shopping mall was built in our city ten years ago, and our city has experienced tremendous economic growth since then. Therefore, most cities in which major shopping malls are built will experience tremendous economic growth shortly afterward.

(E) Most cities that are regional economic hubs contain major shopping malls. A major shopping mall is now being constructed in our city. Therefore, our city will probably become a regional economic hub.

25. Oceanographer: To substantially reduce the amount of carbon dioxide in Earth's atmosphere, carbon dioxide should be captured and pumped deep into the oceans, where it would dissolve. The cool, dense water in ocean depths takes centuries to mix with the warmer water near the surface, so any carbon dioxide pumped deep into oceans would be trapped there for centuries.

Which one of the following is an assumption that the oceanographer's argument requires?

(A) Carbon dioxide will dissolve much more thoroughly if it is pumped into cold water than it will if it is pumped into warmer water.

(B) Evaporation of warmer ocean water near an ocean's surface does not generally release into the atmosphere large amounts of the carbon dioxide dissolved in the evaporating water.

(C) Carbon dioxide dissolved in cool, dense water in ocean depths will not escape back into Earth's atmosphere a long time before the water in which that carbon dioxide is dissolved mixes with warmer water near the surface.

(D) It is the density of the water in the ocean depths that plays the main role in the trapping of the carbon dioxide.

(E) Carbon dioxide should be pumped into ocean depths to reduce the amount of carbon dioxide in the atmosphere only if the carbon dioxide pumped into ocean depths would be trapped there for hundreds of years.

# S T O P

IF YOU FINISH BEFORE TIME IS CALLED, YOU MAY CHECK YOUR WORK ON THIS SECTION ONLY.
DO NOT WORK ON ANY OTHER SECTION IN THE TEST.

SECTION II

Time—35 minutes

27 Questions

<u>Directions:</u> Each set of questions in this section is based on a single passage or a pair of passages. The questions are to be answered on the basis of what is <u>stated</u> or <u>implied</u> in the passage or pair of passages. For some of the questions, more than one of the choices could conceivably answer the question. However, you are to choose the <u>best</u> answer; that is, the response that most accurately and completely answers the question, and blacken the corresponding space on your answer sheet.

*The following passage is adapted from a journal article.*

To understand John Rawls's theory of justice, one first needs to grasp what he was reacting against. The dominant approach in pre-Rawls political philosophy was utilitarianism, which emphasized
(5) maximizing the fulfillment of people's preferences. At first sight, utilitarianism seems plausible—what else should we do but try to achieve the most satisfaction possible for the greatest number of people?—but the theory has some odd consequences. Suppose executing
(10) an innocent person will appease a mob, and that doing so will therefore increase total satisfaction. Incredibly, a utilitarian would have to endorse the execution. Rawls accordingly complains that, in the utilitarian view, there is no reason "why the violation of the
(15) liberty of a few might not be made right by the greater good shared by many."

If we reject utilitarianism and its view about the aim of the good life, how can we know what justice requires? Rawls offers an ingenious answer. He asserts
(20) that even if people do not agree on the aim of the good life, they can accept a fair procedure for settling what the principles of justice should be. This is key to Rawls's theory: Whatever arises from a fair procedure is just.

(25) But what is a fair procedure? Rawls again has a clever approach, beginning with his famous veil of ignorance. Suppose five children have to divide a cake among themselves. One child cuts the cake but does not know who will get which shares. The child is
(30) likely to divide the cake into equal shares to avoid the possibility of receiving the smallest share, an arrangement that the others will also admit to be fair. By denying the child information that would bias the result, a fair outcome can be achieved.

(35) Rawls generalizes the point of this example of the veil of ignorance. His thought experiment features a situation, which he calls the original position, in which people are self-interested but do not know their own station in life, abilities, tastes, or even gender. Under
(40) the limits of this ignorance, individuals motivated by self-interest endeavor to arrive at a solution in which they will not lose, because nobody loses. The result will be a just arrangement.

Rawls thinks that people, regardless of their plan
(45) of life, want certain "primary goods." These include rights and liberties, powers and opportunities, and income and wealth. Without these primary goods, people cannot accomplish their goals, whatever they may be. Hence, any individual in the original position

(50) will agree that everyone should get at least a minimum amount of these primary goods. Unfortunately, this is an inherently redistributionist idea, since the primary goods are not natural properties of human beings. If someone lacks a primary good, it must be provided,
(55) at the expense of others if necessary.

1. According to the passage, Rawls uses which one of the following devices to explain his theory?

   (A) a thought experiment
   (B) a process of elimination
   (C) an empirical study of social institutions
   (D) a deduction from a few basic principles
   (E) a consideration of the meaning of words

2. The purpose of the question in lines 6–8 is to

   (A) point out an implausible feature of utilitarianism
   (B) characterize utilitarianism as internally contradictory
   (C) establish that utilitarianism must be true
   (D) suggest the intuitive appeal of utilitarianism
   (E) inquire into ways of supplementing utilitarianism

3. The author's primary purpose in the passage is to

   (A) show why a once-dominant theory was abandoned
   (B) describe the novel way in which a theory addresses a problem
   (C) sketch the historical development of a celebrated theory
   (D) debate the pros and cons of a complex theory
   (E) argue for the truth of a controversial theory

GO ON TO THE NEXT PAGE.

4. With which one of the following statements would both Rawls and the author of the passage be most likely to agree?

(A) There are situations in which it is permissible to treat the fulfillment of one person's preferences as more important than the fulfillment of the majority's preferences.

(B) Unless individuals set aside their own self-interest, they cannot make fair judgments about the distribution of goods.

(C) If an individual lacks a good, society must sometimes provide that good, even if this means taking it from others.

(D) Most people agree about which of the primary goods is the most valuable.

(E) It is fair to sacrifice the individual's interests if doing so will maximize the satisfaction of the majority.

5. The author's stance toward Rawls's theory is most accurately described as one of

(A) scholarly neutrality with respect both to its objectives and its development

(B) disdain for its pretensions camouflaged by declarations of respect for its author

(C) sympathy with its recommendations tempered with skepticism about its cogency

(D) enthusiasm for its aims mingled with doubts about its practicality

(E) admiration for its ingenuity coupled with misgivings about some of its implications

6. Which one of the following would, if true, most call into question the claim in lines 49–51 of the passage?

(A) Most people value the fulfillment of their own preferences over the fulfillment of the preferences of strangers.

(B) It is impossible in practice for people to be ignorant of their stations in life, abilities, and tastes.

(C) Some people would be willing to risk a complete loss of one primary good for the chance of obtaining an enormous amount of another primary good.

(D) Few people believe that they would be satisfied with only a minimum amount of primary goods.

(E) People tend to overestimate the resources available for distribution and to underestimate their own needs.

GO ON TO THE NEXT PAGE.

*This passage was adapted from an article written by three economists.*

Roughly 40 percent of the African American population of the Southern United States left the South between 1915 and 1960, primarily for the industrial cities of the North. While there was some African
(5) American migration to the North during the nineteenth century, most accounts point to 1915 as the start of what historians call the Great Migration. There were at least three catalysts of the Great Migration. First, World War I increased labor demand in the industrial
(10) North. Second, the war in Europe cut off immigration, which led many Northern employers to send labor agents to recruit African American labor in the South. Finally, a boll weevil infestation ruined cotton crops and reduced labor demand in much of the South in
(15) the 1910s and 1920s.

In short, the Great Migration began in 1915 and not earlier, because it was only then that the North–South income gap became large enough to start such a large-scale migration. Less clear, however, is
(20) why migration continued, and even accelerated, in subsequent decades, at the same time that North–South income differences were narrowing.

We propose that once started, migration develops momentum over time as current migration reduces the
(25) difficulty and cost of future migration. Economists have typically assumed that people migrate if their expected earnings in the destination exceed those of the origin enough to outweigh the difficulties and one-time costs of migration. Previous research
(30) suggests that the difficulties and costs arise from several sources. First, the uncertainty that potential migrants face concerning housing and labor-market conditions in the destination presents a significant hindrance. Second, there is the simple cost in terms of
(35) time and money of physically moving from the origin to the destination. Third, new migrants must familiarize themselves with local labor- and housing-market institutions once they arrive; they must find housing and work, and they must often
(40) adapt to a new culture or language.

Empirical studies show that during the Great Migration, information was passed through letters that were often read by dozens of people and through conversation when migrants made trips back to their
(45) home communities. Thus early migrants provided information about labor- and housing-market conditions to friends and relatives who had not yet made the trip. First-time African American migrants often traveled with earlier migrants returning to the
(50) North after a visit to the South, which reduced physical costs. Additionally, previous migrants reduced new migrants' cost of adapting to a new locale and culture by providing them with temporary housing, food, and even credit. Previous migrants
(55) also provided a cultural cushion for later migrants, so that they did not have to struggle as hard with their new surroundings.

7. Which one of the following most accurately expresses the main point of the passage?

(A) Approximately 40 percent of the African American population left the Southern U.S. between 1915 and 1960—an event historians refer to as the Great Migration.

(B) The Great Migration was triggered by an increased labor demand in the North due to the onset of World War I and a reduced labor demand in the South due to a boll weevil infestation.

(C) Because earlier migrants helped defray the financial costs of migration for later migrants, African American migration to the North accelerated at a time when income differences were narrowing.

(D) In migration movements, earlier migrants reduce the physical costs of moving and provide a cultural and linguistic cushion for later migrants.

(E) Although the Great Migration was initially triggered by the income differential between the North and South, other factors must be cited in order to explain its duration over several decades.

8. According to the passage, the Great Migration did not start earlier than 1915 because

(A) the income gap between the North and South was not large enough to induce people to migrate

(B) the cost of living in the North was prohibitively high before World War I

(C) industrial jobs in the North required specialized training unavailable in the South

(D) previous migration had yet to develop sufficient momentum to induce further migration

(E) agricultural jobs in the South paid very well before the boll weevil infestation

9. The third and fourth paragraphs of the passage function primarily to

(A) cast doubt upon a historical explanation presented in the first paragraph

(B) survey the repercussions of a historical event described in the first two paragraphs

(C) derive a historical model from evidence presented in the first two paragraphs

(D) answer a question raised in the second paragraph about a historical event

(E) provide additional evidence for historical claims made in the first paragraph

GO ON TO THE NEXT PAGE.

10. The authors of the passage would be most likely to agree with which one of the following statements?

    (A) Expected financial gains alone may not be a reliable indicator of the likelihood that an individual will migrate.

    (B) A complete explanation of the Great Migration must begin with an account of what triggered nineteenth-century migrations to the North.

    (C) The Great Migration is not parallel in its broadest patterns to most other known migration movements.

    (D) Most large-scale migrations can be adequately explained in terms of the movement of people from lower- to higher-income regions.

    (E) Large-scale migrations generally did not occur until the early twentieth century, when significant interregional income differences arose as a result of rapid industrialization.

11. The primary purpose of the last sentence of the second paragraph is to

    (A) indicate why previous research on the Great Migration has been misguided

    (B) extend the authors' explanation of the causes of the Great Migration to include later events

    (C) challenge the traditional view that Northern wages were higher than Southern wages prior to 1915

    (D) present a fact about the Great Migration that the authors seek to explain

    (E) suggest that the Great Migration cannot be explained

12. The passage provides the most support for which one of the following statements?

    (A) The highest-paying agricultural jobs in the South prior to 1915 did not pay more than the lowest-paying manufacturing jobs in the North.

    (B) The overall cost of migrating from the South to the North in the twentieth century was lower for the earliest migrants because there were more of the highest-paying jobs available for them to choose from.

    (C) The North–South income gap increased around 1915 because of the increase in demand for labor in the North and the decrease in demand for labor in the South.

    (D) The average wages in the South, though dramatically lower than the average wages in the North, held roughly steady for all workers during the 1910s and 1920s.

    (E) Most migrants in the Great Migration made at least one trip back to the South to provide help and information to other people who were considering migrating as well.

13. Which one of the following, if true, would provide the most support for the authors' analysis of the Great Migration?

    (A) The average amount of time it took new migrants to find employment in the North grew at a steady rate between 1915 and 1960.

    (B) In general, communities of African Americans in the North consisted largely of individuals who shared a common geographic place of origin in the South.

    (C) Housing prices in the North fluctuated between high and low extremes from 1915 to 1960, while housing prices in the South remained relatively constant.

    (D) To maintain a steady rate of recruitment after World War I, Northern employers had to send more and more labor agents to recruit employees in the South.

    (E) There was a large-scale reverse migration of African Americans back to Southern locations later in the twentieth century.

GO ON TO THE NEXT PAGE.

### Passage A

Insider-trading law makes it a crime to make stock transactions, or help others make stock transactions, based on information you have ahead of the general public because of your special position
(5) within a company.

However, trading based on information you have that everyone else doesn't—isn't this part of the very definition of a functioning stock market? The entire field of stock brokering is based on people gaining
(10) knowledge that others don't have and then using it to profit themselves or their clients. If you analyze a stock, decide that it is overvalued, and sell it, you are taking advantage of knowledge that many others don't have. That doesn't make you a criminal; it means
(15) you've done your homework.

Stock markets work best when all the relevant information about a company is spread as widely as possible, as quickly as possible. Stock prices represent a constantly shifting amalgamation of everyone's
(20) information about and evaluations of a company's value. It helps when those who have accurate information about changing circumstances are permitted to act so that stock prices reflect them.

Someone selling a stock because they know
(25) something will happen soon that will lower the stock's value helps spread the knowledge that the price ought to be dropping. Such actions help ensure that stock prices do reflect a more accurate assessment of all the relevant facts. That's good for everyone in the
(30) stock market.

When contemplating insider-trading law, it helps to consider a far more widespread practice: "insider nontrading"—stock sales or purchases that would have been made, but aren't because of inside knowledge.
(35) This is certainly happening every day, and rightfully so. No one would think to lock someone up for it.

### Passage B

One of the basic principles of the stock market is transparency. In a transparent market, information that influences trading decisions is available to all
(40) participants at the same time. Success in the market can then be gained only by skill in analyzing the information and making good investing decisions. In a transparent stock market, everyone has the same chance of making a good investment, and success is
(45) based on individual merit and skill.

In insider-trading situations, some people make investment decisions based on information that other people don't have. People who don't have access to the inside information can't make similarly informed
(50) investment decisions. That unfairly compromises the market: people with inside information can make informed trade decisions far before everyone else, making it difficult or impossible for other people to earn money in the stock market.
(55) This, in turn, causes a loss of investor confidence and could ultimately destroy the market. People invest in the stock market because they believe they can make money. The whole point of capital investments

is to make good investing decisions and make money
(60) over time. If investors believe they can't make money, they won't invest. Undermining investor confidence would thus deny companies access to the funds they need to grow and be successful, and it could ultimately lead to widespread financial repercussions.

14. Both passages are primarily concerned with answering which one of the following questions?

(A) How is insider trading defined?
(B) Should there be severer penalties for insider trading?
(C) Why do investors engage in insider trading?
(D) Is insider trading harmful to the stock market?
(E) What is the best means of regulating insider trading?

15. In their attitudes toward stock trades based on inside information, the author of passage A and the author of passage B, respectively, may be most accurately described as

(A) positive and neutral
(B) positive and negative
(C) neutral and negative
(D) neutral and neutral
(E) negative and negative

16. The authors would be most likely to agree that

(A) insider trading tends to undermine investor confidence in the stock market
(B) all information should be available to all market participants at the same time
(C) it is appropriate for investors to seek to gain an advantage by superior stock analysis
(D) insider nontrading should be regulated to the same extent as insider trading
(E) insider trading is the best means for disseminating information possessed by insiders

GO ON TO THE NEXT PAGE.

17. Which one of the following laws would conform most closely to the position articulated by the author of passage A but not that articulated by the author of passage B?

   (A) a law that prohibits trading based on information that is not shared by everyone

   (B) a law that permits trading based on information gained from analysis of a stock but prohibits trading based on information obtained from one's position within a company

   (C) a law that prohibits trading that could reasonably be expected to undermine investors' confidence in the stock market

   (D) a law that legalizes selling based on inside information that a stock's price ought to be dropping but prohibits buying based on inside information that it should be rising

   (E) a law that legalizes trading based on inside information, as long as that information is not acquired by theft or other unlawful means

18. Passage A, unlike passage B, seeks to advance its argument by

   (A) applying general principles to particular examples

   (B) pointing out similarities between a controversial activity and uncontroversial ones

   (C) describing the consequences that would result from allowing an activity

   (D) showing how a specific activity relates to a larger context

   (E) examining the motivations of an activity's participants

19. The passages' references to the analysis of information about stocks (lines 11–14, lines 40–42) are related in which one of the following ways?

   (A) Passage A presents it as unnecessary, since all relevant information is already reflected in stock prices, whereas passage B presents it as necessary for making sound investment decisions.

   (B) Passage A uses it as an example of an activity that compensates for the market's lack of transparency, whereas passage B uses it as an example of an activity whose viability is conditional upon the transparency of the market.

   (C) Passage A presents it as an activity that gives some investors an unfair advantage over others, whereas passage B presents it as an activity that increases the transparency of the market.

   (D) Passage A presents it as comparable to the acquisition of inside information, whereas passage B contrasts it with the acquisition of inside information.

   (E) Passage A treats it as an option available only to brokers and other stock-market professionals, whereas passage B treats it as an option available to ordinary investors as well.

GO ON TO THE NEXT PAGE.

There are some basic conceptual problems hovering about the widespread use of brain scans as pictures of mental activity. As applied to medical diagnosis (for example, in diagnosing a brain tumor),
(5) a brain scan is similar in principle to an X-ray: it is a way of seeing inside the body. Its value is straightforward and indubitable. However, the use of neuroimaging in psychology is a fundamentally different kind of enterprise. It is a research method the
(10) validity of which depends on a premise: that the mind can be analyzed into separate and distinct modules, or components, and further that these modules are instantiated in localized brain regions. This premise is known as the modular theory of mind.

(15) It may in fact be that neither mental activity, nor the physical processes that constitute it, are decomposable into independent modules. Psychologist William Uttal contends that rather than distinct entities, the various mental processes are likely to be
(20) properties of a more general mental activity that is distributed throughout the brain. It cannot be said, for instance, that the amygdala is the seat of emotion and the prefrontal cortex is the seat of reason, as the popular press sometimes claims. For when I get angry,
(25) I generally do so for a reason. To cleanly separate emotion from reason-giving makes a hash of human experience.

But if this critique of the modular theory of mind is valid, how can one account for the fact that brain
(30) scans do, in fact, reveal well-defined areas that "light up" in response to various cognitive tasks? In the case of functional magnetic resonance imaging (fMRI), what you are seeing when you look at a brain scan is actually the result of a subtraction. The fMRI is
(35) usually interpreted as a map of the rate of oxygen use in different parts of the brain, which stands as a measure of metabolic activity. But what it actually depicts is the differential rate of oxygen use: one first takes a baseline measurement in the control condition,
(40) then a second measurement while the subject is performing some cognitive task. The baseline measurement is then subtracted from the on-task measurement. The reasoning, seemingly plausible, is that whatever remains after the subtraction represents
(45) the metabolic activity associated solely with the cognitive task in question.

One immediately obvious (but usually unremarked) problem is that this method obscures the fact that the entire brain is active in both conditions.
(50) A false impression of neat functional localization is given by differential brain scans that subtract out all the distributed brain functions. This subtractive method produces striking images of the brain at work. But isn't the modular theory of mind ultimately
(55) attractive in part because it is illustrated so well by the products of the subtractive method?

20. Which one of the following most accurately states the main point of the passage?

(A) In spite of troubling conceptual problems surrounding brain scan technology, its use in psychological research on mental activity has grown rapidly.

(B) The use of brain scans to depict mental activity relies on both a questionable premise and a misleading methodological approach.

(C) Contrary to what is usually asserted in the popular press, reason and emotion are probably not located in the prefrontal cortex and the amygdala, respectively.

(D) Although the fMRI is usually interpreted as a measure of metabolic activity in the brain, this interpretation is misguided and therefore leads to false results.

(E) The modular theory of mind has gained wide currency precisely because it is illustrated effectively by the images produced by the subtractive method.

21. According to the modular theory of mind, as described in the passage, mental activity

(A) consists of distinct components in localized areas of the brain

(B) requires at least some metabolic activity in all parts of the brain

(C) involves physical processes over which people have only limited control

(D) is localized in the amygdala and the prefrontal cortex

(E) generally involves some sort of reason-giving

22. The author of the passage would be most likely to agree with which one of the following statements regarding the subtractive method?

(A) Because the subtractive method masks distributed brain functions, empirical results derived using the method are invalid for medical applications.

(B) The subtractive method results in images that strongly support Uttal's view that mental processes are simply properties of a more general mental activity.

(C) Brain scans of individuals experiencing anger that were produced using the subtractive method show that emotions are not actually seated in the amygdala.

(D) The subtractive method seems to strongly support the modular theory of mind because it creates an illusion that brain functions are localized.

(E) The view that the subtractive method depicts differential rates of oxygen use in the brain is based on a fundamental misconception of the method.

GO ON TO THE NEXT PAGE.

23. A central function of the final paragraph of the passage is to

(A) criticize the research results described in the third paragraph on the grounds that they are incompatible with the basic premise described in the first paragraph

(B) suggest that the position articulated in the first paragraph needs to be modified to accommodate the results outlined in the third paragraph

(C) contend that the research method detailed in the third paragraph relies upon an outdated theoretical model described in the second paragraph

(D) argue that the empirical research outlined in the third paragraph points to the inadequacy of the competing views described in the first two paragraphs

(E) show why the type of empirical evidence discussed in the third paragraph does not defeat the argument presented in the second paragraph

24. The author draws an analogy between brain scans and X-rays primarily in order to

(A) contrast a valid use of brain scans with one of more doubtful value

(B) suggest that new technology can influence the popularity of a scientific theory

(C) point to evidence that brain scans are less precise than other available technologies

(D) argue that X-ray images undermine a theory that brain scans are often used to support

(E) show how brain scan technology evolved from older technologies such as X-rays

25. According to the passage, psychologist William Uttal contends that the various mental processes are likely to be

(A) independent modules that are based in different areas of the brain

(B) essentially an amalgamation of emotion and reason

(C) generally uniform in their rates of oxygen use

(D) detectable using brain scans enhanced by means of the subtractive method

(E) features of a general mental activity that is spread throughout the brain

26. Which one of the following statements is most strongly supported by the passage?

(A) Although there are important exceptions, most cognition does in fact depend on independent modules located in specific regions of the brain.

(B) The modular theory of mind holds that regions of the brain that are not engaged in a specific cognitive task have a rate of oxygen use that is close to zero.

(C) During the performance of certain cognitive tasks, the areas of the brain that are most metabolically active show a rate of oxygen use that is higher than that of the rest of the brain.

(D) The baseline measurements of oxygen use taken for use in the subtractive method show that some regions of the brain have high metabolic activity at all times.

(E) When a brain scan subject experiences anger, the subtractive method shows several regions of the brain as "lit up" with metabolic activity.

27. Which one of the following is most analogous to the manner in which fMRI scans of brain activity are typically interpreted, as described in the last two paragraphs?

(A) One particular district in the city voted for the new mayor by an unusually large margin, so the mayor could not have won without that district.

(B) A store launched a yearlong advertising campaign and had an increase in shoppers only during the summer, so the advertisements affected only the summer shoppers.

(C) Much more of the water supply is used by agricultural customers than by residential customers, so it is the agricultural sector that is impacted most severely when droughts occur.

(D) Internet traffic is highest during the evening hours, so most Internet traffic during these peak hours originates in homes rather than in office buildings.

(E) The cheetah is the world's fastest land animal only for short distances, so most cheetahs cannot outrun another land animal over long distances.

# S T O P

IF YOU FINISH BEFORE TIME IS CALLED, YOU MAY CHECK YOUR WORK ON THIS SECTION ONLY.
DO NOT WORK ON ANY OTHER SECTION IN THE TEST.

SECTION III

Time—35 minutes

23 Questions

Directions: Each group of questions in this section is based on a set of conditions. In answering some of the questions, it may be useful to draw a rough diagram. Choose the response that most accurately and completely answers each question and blacken the corresponding space on your answer sheet.

Questions 1–5

A teacher will assign each of five students—Juana, Kelly, Lateefah, Mei, and Olga—to exactly one of two research teams, the green team and the red team. One team will have two members, and the other will have three members. One member of each team will be designated as facilitator. The assignment must satisfy the following conditions:

Juana is assigned to a different team than Olga is.
Lateefah is assigned to the green team.
Kelly is not a facilitator.
Olga is a facilitator.

1. Which one of the following could be an accurate listing of the members and facilitators of the two research teams?

(A)     green team: Juana, Lateefah, Olga (facilitator)
        red team: Kelly, Mei (facilitator)

(B)     green team: Kelly, Lateefah (facilitator), Olga
        red team: Juana, Mei (facilitator)

(C)     green team: Kelly, Lateefah, Olga (facilitator)
        red team: Juana (facilitator), Mei

(D)     green team: Kelly, Mei, Olga (facilitator)
        red team: Juana (facilitator), Lateefah

(E)     green team: Lateefah, Olga (facilitator)
        red team: Juana, Kelly (facilitator), Mei

GO ON TO THE NEXT PAGE.

2. Which one of the following must be true?

   (A)  Juana is assigned to the red team.
   (B)  Lateefah is a facilitator.
   (C)  Olga is assigned to the green team.
   (D)  Juana and Mei are not both facilitators.
   (E)  Neither Juana nor Kelly is a facilitator.

3. Which one of the following must be false?

   (A)  Lateefah is a facilitator, and she is assigned to the same team as Kelly is.
   (B)  Mei is a facilitator, and she is assigned to the same team as Kelly is.
   (C)  Olga is a facilitator, and she is assigned to the same team as Mei is.
   (D)  Lateefah is a facilitator, and she is assigned to a different team than Juana is.
   (E)  Mei is a facilitator, and she is assigned to a different team than Olga is.

4. If Lateefah is a facilitator, then which one of the following could be true?

   (A)  Juana and Kelly are both assigned to the red team.
   (B)  Juana and Mei are both assigned to the red team.
   (C)  Lateefah and Olga are both assigned to the green team.
   (D)  Mei and Olga are both assigned to the green team.
   (E)  Mei and Olga are both assigned to the red team.

5. If Mei is assigned to the green team, then which one of the following must be true?

   (A)  Juana is assigned to the green team.
   (B)  Kelly is assigned to the red team.
   (C)  Olga is assigned to the green team.
   (D)  Lateefah is a facilitator.
   (E)  Mei is a facilitator.

GO ON TO THE NEXT PAGE.

Questions 6–11

An author is planning to write a mystery novel consisting of seven chapters, chapter 1 through chapter 7. Each of seven different clues—R, S, T, U, W, X, and Z—is to be mentioned exactly once, one clue per chapter. The order in which the clues are mentioned is subject to the following constraints:

T cannot be mentioned in chapter 1.

T must be mentioned before W, and there must be exactly two chapters separating the mention of T from the mention of W.

S and Z cannot be mentioned in adjacent chapters.

W and X cannot be mentioned in adjacent chapters.

U and X must be mentioned in adjacent chapters.

6. Which one of the following could be the order in which the clues are mentioned, from the first chapter through the seventh?

(A) S, T, Z, X, U, W, R
(B) T, X, U, W, S, R, Z
(C) U, S, X, T, Z, R, W
(D) X, U, T, Z, R, W, S
(E) Z, R, T, U, X, W, S

GO ON TO THE NEXT PAGE.

7. If X is mentioned in chapter 1, which one of the following could be true?

(A)    R is mentioned in chapter 3.
(B)    R is mentioned in chapter 7.
(C)    S is mentioned in chapter 2.
(D)    W is mentioned in chapter 5.
(E)    Z is mentioned in chapter 3.

8. If U is mentioned in chapter 3, which one of the following could be true?

(A)    R is mentioned in chapter 1.
(B)    R is mentioned in chapter 5.
(C)    S is mentioned in chapter 7.
(D)    W is mentioned in chapter 6.
(E)    X is mentioned in chapter 4.

9. If Z is mentioned in chapter 7, which one of the following could be true?

(A)    R is mentioned in chapter 3.
(B)    S is mentioned in chapter 3.
(C)    T is mentioned in chapter 4.
(D)    U is mentioned in chapter 1.
(E)    X is mentioned in chapter 5.

10. Which one of the following could be true?

(A)    R is mentioned in chapter 7.
(B)    T is mentioned in chapter 5.
(C)    U is mentioned in chapter 7.
(D)    W is mentioned in chapter 3.
(E)    X is mentioned in chapter 6.

11. Which one of the following, if substituted for the constraint that T cannot be mentioned in chapter 1, would have the same effect in determining the order in which the clues are mentioned?

(A)    U cannot be mentioned in chapter 2.
(B)    W cannot be mentioned in chapter 4.
(C)    X cannot be mentioned in chapter 6.
(D)    U must be mentioned in an earlier chapter than T.
(E)    X must be mentioned in an earlier chapter than W.

GO ON TO THE NEXT PAGE.

Questions 12–18

At an upcoming exhibition, four art students—Franz, Greene, Hidalgo, and Isaacs—will each display exactly two paintings—an oil and a watercolor. Exactly two paintings will be displayed on each of the walls of the exhibition room—walls 1, 2, 3, and 4—with one painting in the upper position and one in the lower position. The following conditions will apply:

No wall has only watercolors displayed on it.

No wall has the work of only one student displayed on it.

No wall has both a painting by Franz and a painting by Isaacs displayed on it.

Greene's watercolor is displayed in the upper position of the wall on which Franz's oil is displayed.

Isaacs's oil is displayed in the lower position of wall 4.

12. Which one of the following could be an accurate list of the paintings displayed in the lower position on walls 1 through 4, listed in that order?

(A) Franz's oil, Franz's watercolor, Greene's oil, Isaacs's oil

(B) Franz's oil, Hidalgo's watercolor, Isaacs's watercolor, Isaacs's oil

(C) Greene's oil, Franz's oil, Isaacs's oil, Hidalgo's oil

(D) Hidalgo's oil, Greene's oil, Greene's watercolor, Isaacs's oil

(E) Hidalgo's watercolor, Franz's oil, Greene's oil, Isaacs's oil

GO ON TO THE NEXT PAGE.

13. If Isaacs's watercolor is displayed on wall 2 and Franz's oil is displayed on wall 3, which one of the following must be displayed on wall 1?

   (A) Franz's watercolor
   (B) Greene's oil
   (C) Greene's watercolor
   (D) Hidalgo's oil
   (E) Hidalgo's watercolor

14. If Hidalgo's oil is displayed on wall 2, which one of the following could also be displayed on wall 2?

   (A) Franz's oil
   (B) Greene's watercolor
   (C) Greene's oil
   (D) Hidalgo's watercolor
   (E) Isaacs's watercolor

15. If Greene's oil is displayed on the same wall as Franz's watercolor, which one of the following must be true?

   (A) Greene's oil is displayed in an upper position.
   (B) Hidalgo's watercolor is displayed on the same wall as Isaacs's watercolor.
   (C) Hidalgo's oil is displayed in an upper position.
   (D) Hidalgo's oil is displayed on the same wall as Isaacs's watercolor.
   (E) Isaacs's watercolor is displayed in a lower position.

16. If Franz's oil is displayed on wall 1, which one of the following could be true?

   (A) Franz's watercolor is displayed on wall 4.
   (B) Greene's oil is displayed on wall 2.
   (C) Greene's watercolor is displayed on wall 2.
   (D) Hidalgo's watercolor is displayed on wall 3.
   (E) Isaacs's oil is displayed on wall 1.

17. Which one of the following could be true?

   (A) Both of Franz's paintings and both of Greene's paintings are displayed in lower positions.
   (B) Both of Franz's paintings and both of Greene's paintings are displayed in upper positions.
   (C) Both of Franz's paintings and both of Hidalgo's paintings are displayed in upper positions.
   (D) Both of Greene's paintings and both of Hidalgo's paintings are displayed in lower positions.
   (E) Both of Greene's paintings and both of Hidalgo's paintings are displayed in upper positions.

18. Which one of the following CANNOT be true?

   (A) Franz's watercolor is displayed on the same wall as Greene's oil.
   (B) Franz's watercolor is displayed on the same wall as Hidalgo's oil.
   (C) Greene's oil is displayed in an upper position.
   (D) Hidalgo's watercolor is displayed in a lower position.
   (E) Isaacs's watercolor is displayed on the same wall as Hidalgo's oil.

GO ON TO THE NEXT PAGE.

<u>Questions 19–23</u>

Three real estate companies—RealProp, Southco, and Trustcorp—are considering trading buildings with one another. Each building they own is categorized as either class 1, class 2, or class 3, depending on its approximate value:

 RealProp owns the Garza Tower (class 1), the Yates House (class 3), and the Zimmer House (class 3).

 Southco owns the Flores Tower (class 1) and the Lynch Building (class 2).

 Trustcorp owns the King Building, the Meyer Building, and the Ortiz Building, all of which are class 2.

Each trade must be of exactly one of the following three kinds:

 Trading one building for one other building of the same class

 Trading one class 1 building for two class 2 buildings

 Trading one class 2 building for two class 3 buildings

19. Which one of the following could be the buildings owned by the three companies after only one trade is made?

(A) RealProp: the Flores Tower and the Garza Tower
  Southco: the Lynch Building, the Yates House, and the Zimmer House
  Trustcorp: the King Building, the Meyer Building, and the Ortiz Building

(B) RealProp: the Garza Tower, the King Building, and the Ortiz Building
  Southco: the Flores Tower and the Lynch Building
  Trustcorp: the Meyer Building, the Yates House, and the Zimmer House

(C) RealProp: the Garza Tower and the Lynch Building
  Southco: the Flores Tower, the Yates House, and the Zimmer House
  Trustcorp: the King Building, the Meyer Building, and the Ortiz Building

(D) RealProp: the Garza Tower, the Meyer Building, and the Yates House
  Southco: the Flores Tower and the Lynch Building
  Trustcorp: the King Building, the Ortiz Building, and the Zimmer House

(E) RealProp: the Garza Tower, the Yates House, and the Zimmer House
  Southco: the Lynch Building and the Ortiz Building
  Trustcorp: the Flores Tower, the King Building, and the Meyer Building

GO ON TO THE NEXT PAGE.

20. Which one of the following CANNOT be true, no matter how many trades are made?

   (A)   The buildings owned by RealProp are the Flores Tower and the Garza Tower.
   (B)   The buildings owned by Southco are the Flores Tower and the Meyer Building.
   (C)   The buildings owned by Southco are the Garza Tower and the Lynch Building.
   (D)   The buildings owned by Trustcorp are the Flores Tower and the Ortiz Building.
   (E)   The buildings owned by Trustcorp are the Garza Tower and the Meyer Building.

21. If RealProp owns only class 2 buildings after some number of trades, which one of the following must be true?

   (A)   Trustcorp owns a class 1 building.
   (B)   Trustcorp owns the Meyer Building.
   (C)   Southco owns a class 2 Building.
   (D)   Southco owns both of the class 3 buildings.
   (E)   Southco owns the Flores Tower.

22. If Trustcorp owns no class 2 buildings after some number of trades, which one of the following must be true?

   (A)   RealProp owns a class 1 building.
   (B)   Southco owns only class 2 buildings.
   (C)   Southco has made at least one trade with Trustcorp.
   (D)   Trustcorp owns the Garza Tower.
   (E)   Trustcorp owns the Zimmer House.

23. Which one of the following CANNOT be true, no matter how many trades are made?

   (A)   The buildings owned by RealProp are the Lynch Building, the Meyer Building, and the Ortiz Building.
   (B)   The buildings owned by Southco are the Garza Tower and the Meyer Building.
   (C)   The buildings owned by Southco are the King Building, the Meyer Building, and the Ortiz Building.
   (D)   The buildings owned by Trustcorp are the Flores Tower and the Yates House.
   (E)   The buildings owned by Trustcorp are the Garza Tower and the Lynch Building.

# S T O P

IF YOU FINISH BEFORE TIME IS CALLED, YOU MAY CHECK YOUR WORK ON THIS SECTION ONLY.
DO NOT WORK ON ANY OTHER SECTION IN THE TEST.

SECTION IV

Time—35 minutes

26 Questions

Directions: The questions in this section are based on the reasoning contained in brief statements or passages. For some questions, more than one of the choices could conceivably answer the question. However, you are to choose the best answer; that is, the response that most accurately and completely answers the question. You should not make assumptions that are by commonsense standards implausible, superfluous, or incompatible with the passage. After you have chosen the best answer, blacken the corresponding space on your answer sheet.

1. Community organizer: Before last year's community cleanup, only 77 of the local residents signed up to participate, but then well over 100 actually participated. This year, 85 residents have signed up to participate. Since our community cleanup will be a success if we have at least 100 participants, we can be confident that this year's cleanup will be a success.

The reasoning in the community organizer's argument is most vulnerable to criticism on the grounds that the argument

(A) generalizes about the outcome of an event based on a single observation of a similar situation

(B) takes for granted that people who participated in last year's cleanup will participate this year

(C) confuses a condition that is required for an outcome with one that is sufficient for that outcome

(D) overlooks the possibility that the cleanup will attract participants who are not residents in the community

(E) defines a term in such a way as to ensure that whatever the outcome, it will be considered a positive outcome

2. Bell: Commentators in the media are wrong to criticize the policies Klein implemented. Although her policies are unpopular, they avoided an impending catastrophe. Klein is just the person we need making important decisions in the future.

Soltan: Klein's policies have been effective, but politics matters. In the future, important decisions will need to be made, and she will not have the political support to make them. So she should step down.

Bell and Soltan disagree with each other about which one of the following?

(A) Klein's policies have been effective.
(B) Klein's policies are unpopular.
(C) Klein should step down.
(D) There are important decisions to be made in the future.
(E) Klein's policies were implemented in the face of an impending catastrophe.

3. Psychologist: In our study, participants who were offered the opportunity to purchase a coffee mug were not willing to pay more than $5. If, however, they were given a very similar mug and asked immediately afterwards how much they would be willing to sell it for, most of them held out for more than $5.

Which one of the following, if true, most helps to resolve the apparent discrepancy described above?

(A) A person's assessment of the value of an object depends on his or her evaluation of the inherent properties of the object.

(B) People are usually unable to judge the value of an object when they have possessed it for a long period of time.

(C) The amount a person is willing to spend on an object is determined by the amount that object sold for in the past.

(D) People tend to value an object that they do not own less than they value a very similar object that they already own.

(E) People are more likely to undervalue objects they have been given than objects they have purchased.

GO ON TO THE NEXT PAGE.

4. Ecologist: Before finding a mate, male starlings decorate their nests with fragments of aromatic plants rich in compounds known to kill parasitic insects. Since these parasites are potentially harmful to nestlings, some researchers have hypothesized that the function of these decorations is nestling protection. However, males cease to incorporate such greenery once egg laying starts, which suggests instead that the function of the decorations is to attract females.

Which one of the following, if true, most strengthens the support for the ecologist's conclusion?

(A) Adult starlings are able to defend themselves against parasitic insects.
(B) Male starlings do not decorate their nests in areas with unusually small populations of parasitic insects.
(C) Nestlings grow faster in nests that incorporate aromatic plants than in nests that do not.
(D) Male starlings tend to decorate their nests with a greater number of aromatic plants when a caged female is positioned adjacent to the nest.
(E) The compounds in the aromatic plants used by the male starlings to decorate their nests are harmless to nestlings.

5. A commission has been formed to report on the nation's preparedness for a major natural disaster. The commission's report will not be effective unless the commission speaks with a unified voice. Since individual members of the commission have repeatedly expressed their own opinions about disaster preparedness in the news media well in advance of completion of the report, it will not be effective.

The conclusion of the argument follows logically if which one of the following is assumed?

(A) Commission members who have expressed their opinions about disaster preparedness in the news media have also emphasized their commitment to producing an effective report.
(B) News organizations should not provide a platform for members of the commission to express their opinions about disaster preparedness if doing so will undermine the effectiveness of the commission's report.
(C) The commission will be able to speak with a uniform voice only if individual members' opinions about disaster preparedness are not made public before the report is completed.
(D) If commission members had not expressed their opinions about disaster preparedness in the news media before the report was completed, there would have been much public speculation about what those views were.
(E) The commission's report will not be effective if some of the commission members already had opinions about the nation's disaster preparedness even before the commission was formed.

6. Engineer: Wide roads free of obstructions have been shown to encourage drivers to take more risks. Likewise, a technical fix to slow or reverse global warming by blocking out a portion of the sun's rays would encourage more carbon dioxide emissions, which might cause more global warming in the future.

The engineer's argument can most reasonably be interpreted as invoking which one of the following principles?

(A) Conditions that create a feeling of security also encourage risk taking.
(B) Problems created by humans require human-created solutions.
(C) Technical fixes are inevitably temporary.
(D) Technical fixes cannot discourage risk-taking behavior.
(E) The longer a problem goes unresolved, the worse it becomes.

7. Although some animals exhibit a mild skin reaction to urushiol, an oil produced by plants such as poison oak and poison ivy, it appears that only humans develop painful rashes from touching it. In fact, wood rats even use branches from the poison oak plant to build their nests. Therefore, urushiol probably did not evolve in these plants as a chemical defense.

Which one of the following, if true, adds the most support for the conclusion of the argument?

(A) Wood rats build their nests using dead, brittle branches, not live ones.
(B) A number of different animals use poison oak and poison ivy as food sources.
(C) It is common for plants to defend themselves by producing chemical substances.
(D) In approximately 85 percent of the human population, very small amounts of urushiol can cause a rash.
(E) Poison oak and poison ivy grow particularly well in places where humans have altered natural forest ecosystems.

GO ON TO THE NEXT PAGE.

8. Politician: Some cities have reversed the decay of aging urban areas by providing tax incentives and zoning variances that encourage renovation and revitalization in selected areas. But such legislation should not be commended. Its principal beneficiaries have turned out to be well-to-do professionals who could afford the cost of restoring deteriorating buildings; the long-term residents these programs were intended to help now face displacement due to increased rent and taxes.

Which one of the following principles, if valid, most helps to justify the politician's criticism?

(A) Evaluation of legislation should take into account actual results, not intentions alone.
(B) The wealthier members of a community should not have undue influence on its governance.
(C) A community's tax laws and zoning regulations should apply equally to all individuals within selected areas.
(D) Legislation that is not to anyone's benefit should not be commended.
(E) Laws that give advantage to the well-to-do can also benefit society as a whole.

9. Pundit: It is good to have national leaders voted out of office after a few years. The reason is that reforms are generally undertaken early in a new government. If leaders do not act quickly to solve a problem and it becomes an issue later, then they must either deny that there is a problem or deny that anything could have been done about it; otherwise, they will have to admit responsibility for the persistence of the problem.

Which one of the following most accurately expresses the main conclusion of the pundit's argument?

(A) If national leaders who fail to solve problems are voted out of office after a few years, new leaders will be more motivated to solve problems.
(B) National leaders who stay in power too long tend to deny responsibility for problems that they could have dealt with earlier.
(C) National leaders are most likely to undertake reforms early in a new government.
(D) National leaders who immediately respond to problems upon taking office should be given enough time to succeed at solving them.
(E) National leaders should be removed from office every few years by the voting in of new leaders.

10. Farmer: Agricultural techniques such as crop rotation that do not use commercial products may solve agricultural problems at least as well as any technique, such as pesticide application, that does use such products. Nonetheless, no private for-profit corporation will sponsor research that is unlikely to lead to marketable products. Thus, for the most part, only government-sponsored research investigates agricultural techniques that do not use commercial products.

Which one of the following, if true, most strengthens the farmer's argument?

(A) The government sponsors at least some investigations of agricultural techniques that are considered likely to solve agricultural problems and do not use commercial products.
(B) For almost any agricultural problem, there is at least one agricultural technique that does not use commercial products but that would solve that agricultural problem.
(C) Investigations of agricultural techniques are rarely sponsored by individuals or by any entity other than private for-profit corporations or the government.
(D) Most if not all investigations of agricultural techniques that use commercial products are sponsored by private for-profit corporations.
(E) Most if not all government-sponsored agricultural research investigates agricultural techniques that do not use commercial products.

GO ON TO THE NEXT PAGE.

11.  University spokesperson: Most of the students surveyed
     at the university said they would prefer that the
     current food vendor be replaced with a different
     food vendor next year. Several vendors have
     publicly expressed interest in working for the
     university. For a variety of reasons, however, the
     only alternative to the current vendor is Hall
     Dining Services, which served as the university's
     food vendor up until this past year. Since, other
     things being equal, the preferences of the majority
     of students should be adhered to, we should rehire
     Hall Dining next year.

     The spokesperson's argument is most vulnerable to
     criticism on the grounds that it

     (A)  overlooks the possibility that the students
          surveyed were unaware that only Hall Dining
          Services could be hired if the current vendor
          were not hired
     (B)  relies on a sample that is likely to be
          unrepresentative
     (C)  overlooks the possibility that student preference
          is not the only factor to be considered when it
          comes to deciding which food vendor the
          university should hire
     (D)  overlooks the possibility that there is
          disagreement among students concerning
          the issue of food vendors
     (E)  argues that a certain action ought to be
          undertaken merely on the grounds that it
          would be popular

12.  On average, cats fed canned cat food eat fewer ounces
     of food per day than do cats fed dry cat food; the
     canned food contains more calories per ounce than
     does the dry food. Nonetheless, feeding a cat canned
     cat food typically costs more per day than does feeding
     it dry cat food.

     Which one of the following is most strongly supported
     by the information above?

     (A)  On average, cats fed canned cat food eat more
          calories per day than do cats fed dry cat food.
     (B)  Typically, cats are fed either canned cat food or
          dry cat food, or both.
     (C)  How much it costs to feed a cat a given kind of
          food depends only on how many calories per
          ounce that food contains.
     (D)  On average, it costs no less to feed a cat that
          eats fewer ounces of food per day than it
          does to feed a cat that eats more ounces of
          food per day.
     (E)  Canned cat food typically costs more per ounce
          than does dry cat food.

13.  The Frauenkirche in Dresden, a historic church
     destroyed by bombing in World War II, has been
     reconstructed to serve as a place for church services and
     cultural events. The foundation doing the reconstruction
     took extraordinary care to return the church to its
     original form. It is a puzzle, then, why the foundation
     chose not to rebuild the eighteenth-century baroque
     organ originally designed for the church and instead
     built a modern organ, even though a donor had offered
     to pay the full cost of rebuilding the original.

     Which one of the following, if true, would most help to
     resolve the puzzle described above?

     (A)  An eighteenth-century baroque organ cannot
          adequately produce much of the organ music
          now played in church services and concerts.
     (B)  The organ originally designed for the church
          had some features that modern organs lack.
     (C)  The donation for rebuilding the original
          eighteenth-century baroque organ was
          designated for that purpose alone.
     (D)  By the time the church was destroyed in
          World War II, the eighteenth-century baroque
          organ had been modified several times.
     (E)  In the eighteenth century, the organ played
          an important role in church services at the
          Frauenkirche.

14.  Principle: A government should reduce taxes on imports
     if doing so would financially benefit many
     consumers in its domestic economy. There is a
     notable exception, however: it should never
     reduce import taxes if one or more of its domestic
     industries would be significantly harmed by the
     added competition.

     Conclusion: The government should not reduce taxes on
     textile imports.

     Which one of the following is a statement from which
     the conclusion can be properly drawn using the principle?

     (A)  Reducing taxes on textile imports would not
          financially benefit many consumers in the
          domestic economy.
     (B)  Reducing taxes on textile imports would
          financially benefit some consumers in the
          domestic economy but would not benefit the
          domestic textile industry.
     (C)  The domestic textile industry faces significant
          competition in many of its export markets.
     (D)  The domestic textile industry and consumers in
          the domestic economy would benefit less from
          reductions in taxes on textile imports than they
          would from other measures.
     (E)  The added competition produced by any
          reduction of taxes on imports would
          significantly harm the domestic textile industry.

GO ON TO THE NEXT PAGE.

15. Global warming has contributed to a rise in global sea level not only because it causes glaciers and ice sheets to melt, but also simply because when water is heated its volume increases. But this rise in global sea level is less than it otherwise would be, since over the years artificial reservoirs have been built all around the world that collectively contain a great deal of water that would otherwise reach the sea.

Which one of the following can most reasonably be concluded on the basis of the information above?

(A) The exact magnitude of the rise in global sea level is in dispute.

(B) Rises in global sea level that occurred before the world's reservoirs were built are difficult to explain.

(C) Little is known about the contribution of global warming to the rise in global sea level.

(D) The amount of water in the world's reservoirs is about equal to the amount of water that results from the melting of glaciers and ice sheets.

(E) The amount of water that results from the melting of glaciers and ice sheets cannot be determined by looking at the rise in global sea level alone.

16. Last year, a software company held a contest to generate ideas for their new logo. According to the rules, everyone who entered the contest would receive several prizes, including a T-shirt with the company's new logo. Juan has a T-shirt with the company's new logo, so he must have entered the contest.

The reasoning in the argument is flawed in that the argument

(A) infers a causal relationship when the evidence only supports a correlation

(B) takes a condition that is sufficient for a particular outcome as one that is necessary for that outcome

(C) infers that every member of a group has a feature in common on the grounds that the group as a whole has that feature

(D) has a premise that presupposes the truth of the conclusion

(E) constructs a generalization on the basis of a single instance

17. When expert witnesses give testimony, jurors often do not understand the technical information and thereby are in no position to evaluate such testimony. Although expert witnesses on opposite sides often make conflicting claims, the expert witnesses on both sides frequently seem competent, leaving the jury unable to assess the reliability of their testimonies.

The statements above, if true, most strongly support which one of the following?

(A) There should be limits placed on how much technical information can be considered by both sides in preparing a legal case.

(B) Jury decisions in cases involving expert witness testimonies are not always determined by the reliability of those testimonies.

(C) Jurors who understand the technical information presented in a case can usually assess its legal implications accurately.

(D) Jury members should generally be selected on the basis of their technical expertise.

(E) Expert witnesses who testify on opposite sides in legal cases are likely to agree in their evaluations of technical claims.

18. Tax reformer: The proposed tax reform legislation is being criticized by political groups on the right for being too specific and by political groups on the left for being too vague. Since one and the same statement cannot be both too specific and too vague, the criticisms just go to show that the legislation is framed just as it should be.

Which one of the following is an assumption on which the argument depends?

(A) It is rare for political groups both on the right and on the left to criticize a particular tax reform proposal.

(B) Even an overly specific or vague tax reform proposal can be implemented in a way that produces beneficial results.

(C) The proposed legislation has not been criticized by any group that does not identify itself with the political right or the political left.

(D) The proposed legislation as it is framed was not meant to satisfy either political groups on the right or political groups on the left.

(E) The proposed legislation is not made up of a set of statements some of which are overly specific and some of which are overly vague.

GO ON TO THE NEXT PAGE.

19. Employee: The company I work for has installed
website filtering software that blocks access
to non-work-related websites. It claims that
being able to visit such sites distracts us, keeping
us from doing our best work. But offices that
have windows or are nicely decorated can be
highly distracting too, and no one claims that
people do their best work in an undecorated,
windowless room.

Which one of the following arguments is most similar
in its reasoning to the employee's argument?

(A) Some people advocate moderation in all things.
But different people react differently to certain
substances, so what counts as a moderate
amount of, say, caffeine for you might be too
much for me. So to talk about moderation is
to fail to take into account people's basic
biological differences.

(B) Activists are calling for an electronic device
to be banned, for research has shown that
prolonged exposure to the device while it is in
use causes cancer in laboratory animals. But
most chemicals probably cause cancer when
administered in very high doses, yet no one
would argue that we should ban all these
chemicals for that reason.

(C) Acme expects that approximately 1,000 of
its employees will retire over the next year.
No one would claim that Acme does not need
a work force as large as its present one. So
Acme will need to hire approximately 1,000
people over the next year.

(D) In many creative writing classes, aspiring
writers are told that if the characters they
create are not engaging, their novels and
stories will not sell. But this does not mean
that engaging characters guarantee a sale—
publishers and agents often reject manuscripts
that emphasize character to the exclusion of
other elements.

(E) In the movie industry, a film's success is judged
in terms of its profit relative to its cost. This
is misguided, because under this criterion an
expensive movie that sells just as many tickets
as a lower-budget movie would be less
successful than the lower-budget movie, which
is clearly counterintuitive.

20. At Tromen University this semester, some students
taking French Literature 205 are also taking Biology
218. Every student taking Biology 218 at Tromen is a
biology major. Therefore, some of the students taking
French Literature 205 are not French-literature majors.

The conclusion drawn above follows logically if
which one of the following is assumed to be true at
Tromen University?

(A) French Literature 205 is a required course for
French-literature majors.

(B) Only biology majors are allowed to take
Biology 218.

(C) There are more biology majors than there are
French-literature majors.

(D) There are more French-literature majors than
there are biology majors.

(E) It is not possible to major in both biology and
French literature.

21. Critic: To be a literary classic a book must reveal
something significant about the human condition.
Furthermore, nothing that is unworthy of serious
study reveals anything significant about the
human condition.

If the critic's statements are true, which one of the
following must also be true?

(A) Any book worthy of serious study is a literary
classic.

(B) A book is a literary classic only if it is worthy
of serious study.

(C) There are no literary classics worthy of serious
study.

(D) Some books worthy of serious study do not
reveal anything significant about the human
condition.

(E) Some books that reveal something significant
about the human condition are not literary
classics.

GO ON TO THE NEXT PAGE.

22. Scientists once believed that the oversized head, long hind legs, and tiny forelimbs that characterized *Tyrannosaurus rex* developed in order to accommodate the great size and weight of this prehistoric predator. However, this belief must now be abandoned. The nearly complete skeleton of an earlier dinosaur has recently been discovered. This specimen had the characteristic *T. rex* features but was one-fifth the size and one-hundredth the weight.

The answer to which one of the following questions would most help in evaluating the argument?

(A) Was the ratio of the head size of the recently discovered dinosaur to its body size the same as that for *T. rex*?

(B) At what stage in its life did the recently discovered dinosaur die?

(C) Was *T. rex* the largest and heaviest prehistoric predator?

(D) Was the species to which the recently discovered dinosaur belonged related to *T. rex*?

(E) Did the recently discovered dinosaur prey on species as large as those that *T. rex* preyed on?

23. YXK is currently the television network with the highest overall number of viewers. Among YXK's programs, *Bliss* has the highest numbers of viewers. So *Bliss* currently has more viewers than any other program on television.

The flawed reasoning exhibited by the argument above is most similar to that exhibited by which one of the following?

(A) Soccer players suffer more leg injuries, on average, than any other athletes at this university. Linda Wilson has suffered more leg injuries than any other soccer player at this university. Thus, Linda Wilson is the athlete at this university who has suffered the most leg injuries.

(B) Teachers at our school have won more teaching awards, on average, than teachers at any other school in this city. Janna Patel is the teacher who has won the most awards in the city. So Janna Patel is the best teacher at our school.

(C) The Olson Motor Company manufactures the three best-selling automobile models in the country. The Decade is the Olson Motor Company's best-selling model. Thus, the Decade is the best-selling model in the country.

(D) In this city the highest-paid police officer earns more than the highest-paid firefighter, and the lowest-paid police officer earns more than the lowest-paid firefighter. So in this city police officers earn more, on average, than firefighters do.

(E) *Falling Fast* is the film that is currently earning the most at the box office in the country. The most successful film in the country is typically the one that is showing in the most theaters. So *Falling Fast* is probably the film that is currently showing in the most theaters.

GO ON TO THE NEXT PAGE.

24. A contract between two parties is valid only if one party accepts a legitimate offer from the other; an offer is not legitimate if someone in the position of the party to whom it was made would reasonably believe the offer to be made in jest.

The principle stated above, if valid, most helps to justify the reasoning in which one of the following arguments?

(A)  Joe made a legitimate offer to buy Sandy's car and Sandy has not rejected the offer. Thus, there was a valid contract.

(B)  Kenta accepted Gus's offer to buy a shipment of goods, but Gus, unknown to Kenta, made the offer in jest. Thus, the contract was not valid.

(C)  Frank's offer to buy Mindy's business from her was legitimate. Thus, if Mindy is a reasonable person, she will accept the offer.

(D)  Hai's offer to sell artworks to Lea was made in such a way that no one in Lea's position would have reasonably believed it to be made in jest. Thus, if Lea accepts the offer, they have a valid contract.

(E)  The only offer that Sal made to Veronica was not a legitimate one. Thus, regardless of whether Sal made the offer in jest, there is no valid contract between them.

25. Scientist: A small group of islands near Australia is inhabited by several species of iguana; closely related species also exist in the Americas, but nowhere else. The islands in question formed long after the fragmentation of Gondwana, the ancient supercontinent that included present-day South America and Australia. Thus, these species' progenitors must have rafted on floating debris across the Pacific Ocean from the Americas.

Which one of the following, if true, most weakens the scientist's argument?

(A)  A number of animal species that inhabit the islands are not found in the Americas.

(B)  Genetic analysis indicates that the iguana species on the islands are different in several respects from those found in the Americas.

(C)  Documented cases of iguanas rafting long distances between land masses are uncommon.

(D)  Fossils of iguana species closely related to those that inhabit the islands have been found in Australia.

(E)  The lineages of numerous plant and animal species found in Australia or in South America date back to a period prior to the fragmentation of Gondwana.

26. A recent archaeological find in what was once the ancient kingdom of Macedonia contains the remains of the largest tomb ever found in the region. It must be the tomb of Alexander the Great since he was the greatest Macedonian in history, and so would have had the largest tomb. After all, he conquered an empire that stretched from Greece to much of Asia, though it collapsed after his death.

The reasoning in the argument is most vulnerable to criticism on the grounds that the argument

(A)  takes for granted that greatness can be attained only by military conquest

(B)  takes for granted that the largest tomb found so far must be the largest that was built

(C)  does not show how the recently discovered tomb compares with other tombs from the same period that have been found in other regions

(D)  fails to evaluate the significance of the fact that Alexander's empire did not survive his death

(E)  takes for granted that archaeologists can determine the size of the tomb from its remains

# S T O P

IF YOU FINISH BEFORE TIME IS CALLED, YOU MAY CHECK YOUR WORK ON THIS SECTION ONLY.
DO NOT WORK ON ANY OTHER SECTION IN THE TEST.

Acknowledgment is made to the following sources from which material has been adapted for use in this test booklet:

Dachary Carey, "What's Wrong With Insider Trading?" ©2009 by Life123, Inc.

William J. Carrington, Enrica Detragiache, and Tara Vishwanath, "Migration with Endogenous Moving Costs" in *The Economic Review*. ©1996 by American Economic Association.

"Carrots Dressed as Sticks: An Experiment on Economic Incentives" in *The Economist*. ©2010 by The Economist Newspaper Limited.

Matthew B. Crawford, "The Limits of Neuro-Talk." ©2008 by The New Atlantis.

Brian Doherty, "Free Samuel Waksal" in *Reason Magazine*. ©2002 by Reason Magazine.

David Gordon, "Going off the Rawls" in *The American Conservative*. ©2008 by The American Conservative. http://www.amconmag.com/print.html?Id=AmConservative-2008jul2.

# Wait for the supervisor's instructions before you open the page to the topic.
## Please print and sign your name and write the date in the designated spaces below.
## Time: 35 Minutes

### General Directions

will have 35 minutes in which to plan and write an essay on the topic inside. Read the topic and the accompanying directions carefully. will probably find it best to spend a few minutes considering the topic and organizing your thoughts before you begin writing. In your essay, ure to develop your ideas fully, leaving time, if possible, to review what you have written. **Do not write on a topic other than the one cified. Writing on a topic of your own choice is not acceptable.**

pecial knowledge is required or expected for this writing exercise. Law schools are interested in the reasoning, clarity, organization, uage usage, and writing mechanics displayed in your essay. How well you write is more important than how much you write.

fine your essay to the blocked, lined area on the front and back of the separate Writing Sample Response Sheet. Only that area will be oduced for law schools. Be sure that your writing is legible.

## Both this topic sheet and your response sheet must be turned in to the testing staff before you leave the room.

| Topic Code | Print Your Full Name Here | | |
|---|---|---|---|
| **146379** | Last | First | M.I. |

| Date | Sign Your Name Here |
|---|---|
| **/ /** | |

## Scratch Paper
### Do not write your essay in this space.

# LSAT® Writing Sample Topic

**Directions:** The scenario presented below describes two choices, either one of which can be supported on the basis of the information given. Your essay should consider both choices and argue for one over the other, based on the two specified criteria and the facts provided. There is no "right" or "wrong" choice: a reasonable argument can be made for either.

Tony, a beer brewer, is deciding whether to start a production brewery—a brewery that brews, packages, and distributes specialty beer to be sold at other locations—or to start a brewpub—a full-service restaurant that serves specialty beer brewed on-site. Using the facts below, write an essay in which you argue for one option over the other based on the following two criteria:

- Tony wants to develop a reputation among beer critics and connoisseurs for producing high-quality beer.
- Tony wants to be able to devote time and resources to the development of new beer offerings.

A production brewery would be able to distribute its products to a large geographic area. In order to get the brewery's beers to be carried in stores or offered at bars, Tony would need to put time into sales and marketing. There are already a large number of breweries that distribute to the area. A production brewery's products are likely to be reviewed by beer critics. A production brewery would initially need to focus on a small number of core offerings. If these proved to be popular, Tony would be able to introduce a series of experimental, limited-edition beer offerings.

A brewpub would draw most of its customers from the local area, which has few brewpubs. Tony would need to oversee the day-to-day operations of the restaurant side of the business. Tony might be able to eventually hire a restaurant manager. Many customers at brewpubs are interested primarily in the food. Brewpubs are more likely to be reviewed by restaurant critics rather than beer critics. Beer connoisseurs enthusiastically seek out brewpubs, and share information about brewpubs on social media. Tony would interact directly with customers at a brewpub. Brewpubs brew batches of beer in relatively small volumes and can rotate their offerings relatively quickly.

WPAA14

# Scratch Paper
## Do not write your essay in this space.

# COMPUTING YOUR SCORE

## Directions:

1. Use the Answer Key on the next page to check your answers.

2. Use the Scoring Worksheet below to compute your raw score.

3. Use the Score Conversion Chart to convert your raw score into the 120–180 scale.

## Scoring Worksheet

1. Enter the number of questions you answered correctly in each section.

|  | Number Correct |
|---|---|
| SECTION I................ | _____ |
| SECTION II............... | _____ |
| SECTION III.............. | _____ |
| SECTION IV ............. | _____ |

2. Enter the sum here: _____

**This is your Raw Score.**

## Conversion Chart
### For Converting Raw Score to the 120–180 LSAT Scaled Score
### LSAT Form 6LSN121

| Reported Score | Raw Score Lowest | Raw Score Highest |
|---|---|---|
| 180 | 100 | 101 |
| 179 | 99 | 99 |
| 178 | 98 | 98 |
| 177 | 97 | 97 |
| 176 | * | * |
| 175 | 96 | 96 |
| 174 | 95 | 95 |
| 173 | 94 | 94 |
| 172 | 93 | 93 |
| 171 | 92 | 92 |
| 170 | 90 | 91 |
| 169 | 89 | 89 |
| 168 | 87 | 88 |
| 167 | 86 | 86 |
| 166 | 84 | 85 |
| 165 | 83 | 83 |
| 164 | 81 | 82 |
| 163 | 79 | 80 |
| 162 | 77 | 78 |
| 161 | 76 | 76 |
| 160 | 74 | 75 |
| 159 | 72 | 73 |
| 158 | 70 | 71 |
| 157 | 68 | 69 |
| 156 | 66 | 67 |
| 155 | 64 | 65 |
| 154 | 62 | 63 |
| 153 | 61 | 61 |
| 152 | 59 | 60 |
| 151 | 57 | 58 |
| 150 | 55 | 56 |
| 149 | 53 | 54 |
| 148 | 51 | 52 |
| 147 | 50 | 50 |
| 146 | 48 | 49 |
| 145 | 46 | 47 |
| 144 | 44 | 45 |
| 143 | 43 | 43 |
| 142 | 41 | 42 |
| 141 | 40 | 40 |
| 140 | 38 | 39 |
| 139 | 37 | 37 |
| 138 | 35 | 36 |
| 137 | 34 | 34 |
| 136 | 33 | 33 |
| 135 | 32 | 32 |
| 134 | 30 | 31 |
| 133 | 29 | 29 |
| 132 | 28 | 28 |
| 131 | 27 | 27 |
| 130 | 26 | 26 |
| 129 | 25 | 25 |
| 128 | 24 | 24 |
| 127 | 23 | 23 |
| 126 | 22 | 22 |
| 125 | * | * |
| 124 | 21 | 21 |
| 123 | 20 | 20 |
| 122 | 18 | 19 |
| 121 | * | * |
| 120 | 0 | 17 |

*There is no raw score that will produce this scaled score for this form.

# ANSWER KEY

## SECTION I

| | | | | | | | |
|---|---|---|---|---|---|---|---|
| 1. | D | 8. | C | 15. | C | 22. | D |
| 2. | A | 9. | D | 16. | B | 23. | E |
| 3. | A | 10. | D | 17. | E | 24. | E |
| 4. | E | 11. | D | 18. | D | 25. | C |
| 5. | A | 12. | C | 19. | A | | |
| 6. | B | 13. | A | 20. | A | | |
| 7. | D | 14. | C | 21. | B | | |

## SECTION II

| | | | | | | | |
|---|---|---|---|---|---|---|---|
| 1. | A | 8. | A | 15. | B | 22. | D |
| 2. | D | 9. | D | 16. | C | 23. | E |
| 3. | B | 10. | A | 17. | E | 24. | A |
| 4. | A | 11. | D | 18. | B | 25. | E |
| 5. | E | 12. | C | 19. | D | 26. | C |
| 6. | C | 13. | B | 20. | B | 27. | B |
| 7. | E | 14. | D | 21. | A | | |

## SECTION III

| | | | | | | | |
|---|---|---|---|---|---|---|---|
| 1. | C | 8. | B | 15. | D | 22. | E |
| 2. | D | 9. | D | 16. | B | 23. | D |
| 3. | D | 10. | A | 17. | E | | |
| 4. | E | 11. | B | 18. | D | | |
| 5. | B | 12. | A | 19. | C | | |
| 6. | D | 13. | A | 20. | A | | |
| 7. | E | 14. | E | 21. | A | | |

## SECTION IV

| | | | | | | | |
|---|---|---|---|---|---|---|---|
| 1. | A | 8. | A | 15. | E | 22. | B |
| 2. | C | 9. | E | 16. | B | 23. | A |
| 3. | D | 10. | C | 17. | B | 24. | E |
| 4. | D | 11. | A | 18. | E | 25. | D |
| 5. | C | 12. | E | 19. | B | 26. | B |
| 6. | A | 13. | A | 20. | E | | |
| 7. | B | 14. | E | 21. | B | | |

# LSAT® PREP TOOLS

# The Official LSAT SuperPrep II™

SuperPrep II contains everything you need to prepare for the LSAT—a guide to all three LSAT question types, three actual LSATs, explanations for all questions in the three practice tests, answer keys, writing samples, and score-conversion tables, plus invaluable test-taking instructions to help with pacing and timing. SuperPrep has long been our most comprehensive LSAT preparation book, and SuperPrep II is even better. The practice tests in SuperPrep II are PrepTest 62 (December 2010 LSAT), PrepTest 63 (June 2011 LSAT), and one test that has never before been disclosed.

With this book you can

• Practice on genuine LSAT questions

• Review explanations for right and wrong answers

• Target specific categories for intensive review

• Simulate actual LSAT conditions

LSAC sets the standard for LSAT prep—and SuperPrep II raises the bar!

**Available at your favorite bookseller.**

LSAC.org